Building Support for Your School

How to Use Children's Work to Show Learning

Judy Harris Helm

Amanda Helm

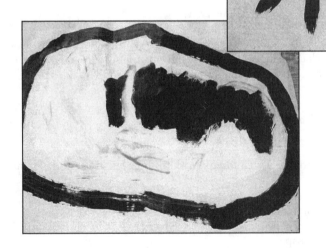

TEACHERS COLLEGE PRESS

Teachers College, Columbia University
New York and London

This book is dedicated to Anna Marie Harris, mother of Judy and grand-mother of Amanda, who passed away during the writing of this book. Even though she was a traditional mother she encouraged us to be all we could be, to develop our intellect and to reach for our dreams. She gave her children and grandchildren both roots and wings. Her spirit lives on in our work.

Published by Teachers College Press, 1234 Amsterdam Avenue, New York, NY 10027

Library of Congress Cataloging-in-Publication Data

Helm, Judy Harris.
  Building support for your school : how to use children's work to show learning / Judy Helm and Amanda Helm.
    p. cm.
  Includes bibliographical references and index.
  ISBN-13: 978-0-8077-4714-8 (pbk. : alk. paper)
  ISBN-10: 0-8077-4714-9 (pbk. : alk. paper)
  1. Communication in education. 2. Advocacy advertising. I. Helm, Amanda. II. Title.
  LB1033.5.H45 2006
  639.2'9371–dc22   2006008728

ISBN-13: 978–0–8077-4714-8 (paper)

ISBN-10: 0–8077-4714-9 (paper)

Printed on acid-free paper
Manufactured in the United States of America

13   12   11   10   09   08   07   06   8   7   6   5   4   3   2   1

Contents

Preface

MOTHERS AND THEIR GROWN DAUGHTERS have much to talk about. It is rare when these conversations include in-depth applications of their chosen areas of advanced study, especially when they are divergent. That is, however, exactly what happened in the Helm family. This book is the result of a collaboration of a mother, Judy, who provides consulting and training of teachers and her daughter, Amanda, who has worked in the world of newspapers and public relations and who now studies and teaches marketing in a university. Although there were many previous family conversations about the importance of active, engaged learning and many projects that occurred in the Helm house, it was not until a recent Thanksgiving vacation that the benefit of "putting our heads together" became apparent. The family conversation turned to the difficulties of sharing the value of project work with laypersons.

Although Judy saw wonderful project work and found that teachers and administrators could document and collect evidence of learning, they often did not have the skills or the confidence to share this in meaningful ways. Conclusive evidence of children's learning was often buried under pages of words that no one had the patience to read or lost in a colorful display that emphasized fun, not learning. Teachers were often overwhelmed with having to teach "standards" even as they had multiple powerful examples of children achieving those standards in their classrooms. This challenge became even more important with an increase in emphasis on test scores and accountability. Although many education personnel deplored the fact that all the children

learned and accomplished was often reduced to one score on one test, very little was being done to provide additional evidence of learning or to process that evidence and share it in a meaningful way.

The Thanksgiving conversation evolved into a joint study of communication pieces (displays, newsletters, notes sent to a child's home) about children's learning that had been collected. Amanda shared how professional communicators in marketing, public relations, and museumology think about the communication process. We shared with teachers and directors the importance of strategic communication and studied their displays and project work. The more we studied what was happening in education communications, the more we saw golden opportunities missed. There were many times that strong statements to parents, other educators, and the community could have been made about what students were actually learning in schools. In some cases, educators unknowingly were sending a message that was the very opposite of what they wanted to say! At the same time, we were hesitant to bring up another job for those on the front lines of education. However, we realized as we studied school communications that it is frontline professionals who have the most credibility and the greatest opportunity to collect and present evidence. Our challenge was to provide knowledge and skills that would result in professional communications but that could be learned quickly. We also had to find ways to save time. Together we experimented with templates, checklists, and other time savers to help educators incorporate children's work and become confident and accurate communicators. This collaboration resulted in the book you are about to read.

In Part I, Opening Windows, we look at the challenges that schools face today in communication and the power of evidence of student learning to help meet those challenges. We present the need for educators to be advocates of schools, to communicate well, and to think like communicators. Schools and all other institutions involved in education, such as museums or community agencies, must be able to clearly delineate their educational goals and then show others achievement of those goals. We share what professional communicators know about communication and how the sharing of evidence of educational processes can improve support for quality education.

In Part II, Strategies for Becoming Educator-Communicators, we introduce a model of the communication process as viewed by professional communicators. Then seven strategies that educator-communicators can use to take communication off autopilot and to get a clear, consistent message out about student learning are introduced, each in a separate chapter. We integrate research from graphic design and from museum and media professionals with specific ideas that can easily be applied by educators in early childhood centers, schools, and community education centers.

We also share how to reach out to media such as radio, television, and newspapers to increase the chances of getting your message out.

Part III, Resources for Educator-Communicators, has two chapters. Chapter 11, Foundation Builders, provides specific guidance as educational personnel engage in the process of thinking strategically about communication, including analyzing their audience and providing support for professional communication within their programs. Chapter 12, Tools for Opening Windows, contains time savers and directions for communication ideas incorporating student work that can be used by any educational institution to look professional and to effectively demonstrate what students are learning in their programs. The last "tool" is a list of additional resources that we have found helpful.

WE ARE HOPEFUL that our collaboration will cause you, the reader, to take a serious look at the messages you are sending. How do you communicate about your program? What image do others have of your center, school, or program? What wonderful treasures of student work can you reveal? We are hoping that our work together will open windows for you so that you may in turn open windows for others into your classrooms and programs.

Acknowledgments

The AUTHORS ARE VERY GRATEFUL for the hard work, support, encouragement, and enthusiasm of many teachers in the field for the development of this book. We can't ever repay Northminster Learning Center—especially Stacy Berg, Executive Director, Pam Scranton, Educational Coordinator, and teacher Lora Taylor for their support. Their generosity in sharing their work and trying out our ideas has been immensely valuable in making this book practical. They are both our co-workers and our inspiration. We also wish to thank all those who contributed work to the book for our use. This includes the Chicago Children's Museum, University Primary School, Rebecca Wilson and the West Liberty Dual Language program, Brenda Dexter, DeCarla Burton, Pat Fontroy, Kathy Steinheimer and Rock Island Head Start program. The authors are especially appreciative of their editor, Susan Liddicoat. Without her immense patience and encouragement, this book would not have happened.

PART I

Opening Windows

CHAPTER 1

Opening Windows into Schools: Today's Communication Challenges

It is a Saturday morning. The 2nd-grade teacher is drinking her second cup of coffee and reading the morning newspaper—two activities she rarely gets to enjoy during the week. When she opens the paper to the editorial pages, her attention is riveted by a letter to the editor blasting schools and teachers. It is another call for more testing and proof that children are learning in the schools. Of course, the author of the letter claims that children are not learning anything in classrooms. Too much "investigating" and "inquiry." There is not enough reading, writing, and arithmetic. He calls for a return to memorization, drill and practice, and standardized group achievement tests to measure teacher effectiveness.

The teacher sighs. Children are learning in her classroom—she knows that. This week they have been studying farming and the harvest. The children were fascinated by the combine and other big farm machinery. They had interviewed the owner of a farm equipment company and visited the field where combines were running. They were reading about harvest, writing about harvest, and drawing and labeling parts of the equipment. They were doing research on the Internet and writing letters to find answers to their questions. They were working together. When the teacher introduced the concept of building models to scale, children began using math skills that were at a higher level than the 2nd-grade book. Students were willingly doing more math problems than she ever would have assigned. Her classroom was filled with farm machinery manuals, textbooks for older children about farming and crops, and encyclopedias—authentic literature that they were motivated to read.

Of course, her children need lots of practice and lots of direct instruction in skills. She knows that and provides that. However, they also need opportunities to learn about things that interest them, to discover the joy of finding the answer to questions, and to have the opportunity to use those new academic skills that they are learning in the more structured part of her school day. Reluctantly, she realized that this harvest project was probably exactly the kind of learning experience this letter writer had so scathingly criticized.

The trouble is, she thought, that this letter writer just doesn't understand. The writer has probably never seen the learning that happens when children are motivated and engaged. There is so much more than test scores! He thinks they provide the only evidence that students are learning! He should just visit my classroom, she thought. I could give him evidence. I could *show him* how children are learning the basics and more. But how would I get the evidence to him. How could I ever get this letter writer to come into our world and see what really happens? He would never come to our school, she thinks, and I don't know how to bring it to him. With another sigh she turns the page, giving up.

CHALLENGES TO SCHOOLS

WORKING HARD, OFTEN AGAINST CHALLENGES such as increasing class sizes, decreasing parental involvement and increasing student diversity, teachers are rightfully frustrated at the criticisms they receive about their educational practices. Many teachers and other school personnel have had thoughts and experiences similar to those of the teacher in the introduction. Schools where children are doing poorly are generally schools located where families are facing challenges of poverty, single parenting, and inadequate child care. However, critics often focus narrowly on test scores and simplistic solutions. The increasing dependence on standardized testing as a measure of school effectiveness, the emphasis on early direct instruction in reading and numeracy put educators on the defensive. Criticisms often reveal a lack of understanding of the considerable changes that have occurred in schools and families since the 1950s or the restrictions and challenges that exist for school personnel today. Yet educators know that this emphasis on assessment or "back-to-basics" teaching provides insufficient guidance for making changes in the actual learning experiences that teachers provide in the classroom.

On the other hand, educators, along with the general public, are aware that some children are not doing well in school. Large numbers of school-age children, including children from all social classes, have significant difficulties in learning to read. However, failure to learn to read adequately for continued school success is much more likely among poor children, among non-White children, and among nonnative speakers of English (Snow, Burns, & Griffin, 1998). Although strides are being made in improving the reading scores of these children, they continue to lag behind their peers. Low scores nationwide in reading achievement (Donahue, Finnegan, Lutkus, Allen, & Campbell, 2000) and in math problem solving have fueled a general anxiety about educational practices. Although this 2nd-grade teacher may have students who are mastering reading and writing and are excited about learning, this may not be true for other classrooms in her community. The writer of the letter to the editor may be expressing concerns shared by many members of the community locally and certainly many across the country. If the teacher and the author of the letter had an opportunity to sit down and talk, they doubtless would find that they have common goals and common concerns.

It is also feasible that the letter writer does not have an accurate and complete picture of what is occurring in schools in his neighborhood and community. In an age when weather information can be obtained instantly and news events around the world are reported immediately after they happen, knowledge about what goes on in the school down the street is still a mystery to many members of the tax-paying community. In addition, since most adults have been through a school system, they believe they already have an understanding of what occurs there. This understanding may or may not be up to date and accurate. Clearly the situation could be improved with communication. If teachers and administrators were more proactive in the communication process, they would increase the likelihood that the vision citizens had of their schools was accurate. The result would be more support of schools and more effective education as members of the community became more involved in their schools.

The Need for Advocacy

Increasingly those in education are feeling more and more compelled to advocate for best practices for children in a variety of settings. Funding agencies, including the federal and state governments, have become increasingly directive about educational decisions, dictating what curriculum should be in schools, how programs such as bilingual education should be organized, and what textbooks and other materials are to be used in classrooms. Professional educators, as interpreters of research and other information about learning, are finding that part of their role as professionals is to define and articulate best practices for children and families that will lead to informed decision making. Teachers, principals, directors of centers, and other educators are discovering the necessity of clear communication with decision makers, such as legislators and board members, as key decisions are being made, so they have a realistic understanding of the long-term effect of their decisions.

Accountability and program evaluation have begun to dominate school processes. Funding of schools is under scrutiny along with all other government expenditures. Effectiveness is more closely monitored than in the past, and there are requirements for informing constituencies of school programs of their effectiveness, even at the preschool and primary levels. Funding is being linked to school success. The introduction of school choice has created a need for schools to communicate what children are learning in their schools and the credibility of their programs. In some communities, access to funds is a critical issue for the survival of these schools. Community education programs such as those offered by social service agencies and community organizations are also finding they have to show results to compete for students and funding.

Unfortunately, this demand for accountability is currently focused on standardized achievement test scores. Although there are problems with standardized group-administered achievement tests at all age levels, they are especially problematic for children of preprimary and primary ages. Young children do not do well filling in bubbles on computerized forms. They also do not reliably perform well in on-demand tests. These tests usually have content that is abstract, that requires extensive verbal abilities, and that is potentially biased against children who are unfamiliar or uncomfortable with testlike activities and with middle-class manners and mores. These limitations have made it difficult to show what children are learning through testing.

The push for accountability does not stop with schools. Early childhood centers are under increasing pressure from parents and funding agencies to demonstrate that children are "ready to learn" when they enter school. Parents often hear "horror stories" of children not being admitted to prestigious private schools. They begin to worry that their child may be falling behind, even at 2 or 3 years of age.

Preschool programs and childcare centers are sometimes compared based on the number of completed papers children bring home or the number of ABCs children can recite. Sometimes high-quality early childhood centers, where children are engaged in concrete hands-on educational experiences and are learning to use literacy in meaningful ways, lose children from their programs because the parents interpret the lack of dittos coming home as a lack of evidence that children are learning.

On the other hand, technology has created a new information age for parents. Some parents have access to recent research reports and information on new educational methods on the Internet. Parents are sometimes aware before educators of new research. Advances such as brain scans and analyses of neurochemistry have changed concepts about how the brain develops, how information is processed, and how learning occurs. This is changing ideas about how children learn and the most effective ways to teach. Concerned parents are demanding evidence that learning experiences are intellectually stimulating and build not only basic skills but skills needed in the 21st century, such as mastery of technology, problem solving, and working collaboratively with groups of students.

There are a number of institutions in our communities besides schools and early childhood centers that provide educational services to children and families. These include religious organizations, youth groups, libraries, and museums. These programs usually rely on community funding or foundation grants to maintain their programs. Increasingly, these programs have been questioned about the value of their services or the effectiveness of their approaches to education, just as the writer of the letter to the editor questioned the schools. Enrollment in voluntary programs decreases when the participants do not see the value of the experience, especially if they have to pay a fee.

The ultimate in the power and influence of test scores and the impact these have on schools and communities is the use of test scores to determine in which communities to live. Real estate agents regularly have this information available for prospective property buyers.

Evidence of Children's Learning

Test scores are not the only way to provide evidence of children's learning and to make judgments about effectiveness. If a program is successfully teaching children to read, to write, to do scientific and mathematical thinking, and to understand how their communities and governments work, then there should be ample evidence by looking at a student's daily ongoing work. For example, the behavior and products of a child who can read a book about early settlers, discuss the challenges they faced, and write about the Oregon Trail are strong evidence of the child's learning and in many ways more valuable evidence than a test score. The goal, after all, is not to create good test takers but to prepare children who will have the skills and knowledge to function successfully in society, to become good citizens, and to be able to complete goals.

There is, in fact, much evidence in schools that children *are* learning. In many schools this evidence is carefully documented, collected, and analyzed. It provides insight for teachers about what children do and do not know and assists in instructional planning. It also enables differentiation of who is and who is not learning. This evidence of learning is gathered using checklists based on national standards and in carefully controlled collections of children's work. It is collected as part of authentic performance assessment systems such as the Work Sampling System. These systems are accurate measures of children's achievement. Children who are judged to be performing well on the Work Sampling System, which bases decisions on this type of evidence, also do well on standardized tests (Meisels, Bickel, Nicholson, Xue and Atkins-Burnett, 2001).

Sometimes group-administered standardized tests actually present an inaccurate view of performance. This can happen when the test covers concepts or experiences not familiar to the students, especially if they are from cultural or language minority groups. Tests can also indicate that a school is not performing up to a normative nationwide standard when, in fact, the school has made enormous progress in achievement.

Viewing samples of student work and sharing student accomplishments can refocus the community on the positive results. Sometimes a work product can capture the impact of a learning experience in ways that no test scores can. Figure 1.1 is an example of a time 1 and time 2 documentation of a child's experience learning about fire trucks in Pam Scranton's preschool classroom.

THE POWER OF DOCUMENTATION

The collection and sharing of student work, such as the time 1 and time 2 drawings, is called *documenta-*

Figure 1.1. Two examples of fire truck drawings. These drawings by 4-year-old David were made 2½ weeks apart during a study of a fire truck. The documentation captures not only changes in his knowledge about fire trucks but also his ability to use pencil and paper for representation and his use of letters.

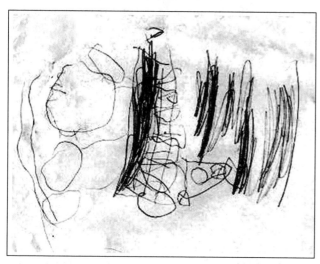

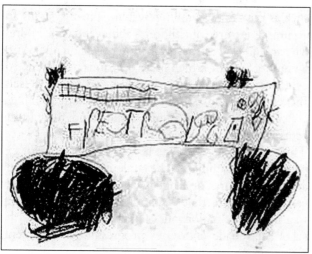

tion (Helm, Beneke, & Steinheimer, 1997, 1998b). Documentation is simply "the provision of evidence." The *American Heritage Dictionary of the English Language* (2000), defines *to document* as:

> 2. To support (an assertion or a claim, for example) with evidence or decisive information.

Documentation in schools is the provision of evidence of student learning. Through comprehensive, careful, systematic documentation of the learning that occurs when children are involved in informal, engaging, and meaningful learning experiences, schools can meet the demands for both effective teaching and accountability. Through documentation, the teacher can make it possible for others to "see" the learning that takes place. Documentation also provides the evidence needed for reliably assessing children's progress, for meeting accountability requirements, for monitoring individual students' growth and development, and for evaluating programs. In contrasting documentation with achievement tests, Helm and colleagues (1998b) state that good quality documentation can do the following:

- Provide evidence of children's learning and progress in all areas of a child's development: physical, emotional, social, and cognitive
- Offer insight into complex learning experiences when teachers use an integrated approach
- Emphasize learning as an interactive process by documenting what children learn through active exploration and interaction with adults, other children, and materials
- Show the advantages of activities and materials that are concrete, real, and relevant to the lives of young children, as opposed to abstract, artificial events like group testing situations
- Enable the teacher to assess what a child knows or can do so the teacher can increase the difficulty, complexity, and challenge of an activity as children are involved with it and as they develop understanding and skills. (p. 24)

Purposes of Documentation

When documentation is used in a program, it is usually collected, analyzed, and shared for the following purposes:

- Guiding instruction
- Assessing children
- Studying pedagogy

When documentation is used for the purpose of *guiding instruction* it is ongoing and reflection on documentation is immediate. Teachers listen, observe, and examine children's work. Teachers take photographs of children in the process of learning and write anecdotal notes of their observations. They may collect and examine children's products, such as drawings and constructions, that the children have created that day. When this documentation is examined and reflected upon during the learning process, it is often not displayed. If it is displayed, it is usually simply stuck on a bulletin board for reflection. This documentation is often referred to as raw documentation. It shapes the direction of projects and learning experiences during the process.

When documentation is used for the purpose of *assessing children*, evidence is gathered about the knowledge, skills, and dispositions of individual children. Assessment enables the teacher to be sure that each child is learning what he or she needs to learn to be successful in school. It provides information on what each child does and does not know and can and cannot do. Documentation is part of an authentic assessment process that uses children's performance in activities that occur on a daily basis.

Authentic performance assessment uses quality documentation, including children's work samples collected into portfolios, photographic or video recordings, and observations. There is often a development checklist or a standards checklist that teachers use to document growth and development of each child's skills over a specific time. There are many different approaches to authentic performance assessment (Dichtelmiller, Jablon, Dorfman, Marsden, & Meisels, 1997; Gardner, 1993; Gronlund & Engel, 2001; Gullo, 2005; Meisels, 1995). Systematic and focused authentic assessments have been found to be reliable and valid. For example, as noted earlier, studies of the Work Sampling System have shown that teachers' judgments of performance using it correlate well with a standardized, individually administered, psychoeducational battery; that it is a reliable predictor of achievement ratings in kindergarten–grade 3; and that it correctly identifies children at risk (Meisels et al., 2000).

Another purpose of documentation is to provide insight into the teaching and learning process. When documentation is collected and studied for the purpose of understanding these processes, it is sometimes called *pedagogical documentation* (Dahlberg, Moss, & Pence, 1999). Pedagogical documentation is a major compo-

nent of the philosophy of the well-known preschools in Reggio Emilia, Italy, where reflection and in-depth documentation shape their pedagogy and are the major source of professional growth and development (Rinaldi, 2001). An excellent example of pedagogical documentation in U.S. schools and centers is *Rearview Mirror: Reflections of a Preschool Car Project* (Beneke, 1998). Through the documentation of the exploration of a car by a group of preschool children, the teachers and the staff of the center were able to reflect on the pedagogical decisions and the value of the learning experience for the children.

In busy classrooms it is often difficult for teachers to have time to observe and reflect on their teaching. Capturing and preserving what is happening enables teachers to study the nature of children and learning, the validity of the decisions that they make in the process of teaching, and the value of the learning experiences they provide.

An additional purpose of documentation and the focus of this book is the use of documentation as a vehicle for *communication* about centers and schools. This communication occurs among staff members, with children about their work, with parents about what their children are learning in their classrooms, and with the members of the greater community. When documentation is used in this way, the educators open windows into the heart of the classroom and develop respect, understanding, and support for the work being done there (Helm et al., 1998b). When educators fulfill this role, we call them *educator-communicators*. There is much potential for the use of documentation for communication to impact what happens to schools and centers today.

Documentation that is shared outside the immediate education environment is referred to as *processed* or *published documentation*. It is selected, organized, and displayed with careful attention to who will be viewing the documentation and to the communication goals. "The Bee Project History Book" by teacher Lora Taylor is an example of documentation that has been processed or published for communication (see Figure 1.2). Ms. Taylor has used the left-hand pages of the book to communicate with parents about the project approach method. On the right-hand pages are photos that parents can talk about with their children. Published documentation also may be in the form of panels, media presentations, website pages, newsletter articles, and displays.

Figure 1.3 summarizes the purposes of documentation, listing the different types of documentation

Figure 1.2. Bee Project book. Children take turns bringing this project history book home to share with parents. The left page (top) communicates information about the project approach as a teaching method. The right page (bottom) presents photos and children's work along with a narrative of the project.

During phase two project work, children became very concerned with detail. As their understanding of something deepens, it becomes important to remember details about that and organize new information. As they added each new part to the bee diagram, it was important that it represent the true characteristic of the bee, it was important that the part was placed on the correct place on the body, and that it was labeled with the correct word.

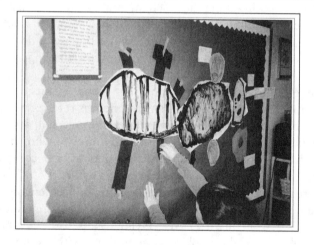

During Learning Centers, a small group of children worked to make a bee diagram using everyday art materials, such as paper, glue, and paint. They wanted to represent the many details of the bee, such as stripes, wings, and pollen on the legs. Then, they labeled the body parts using developmental writing. When the diagrams were all finished, the children wrote a story about the bee and its adventures.

Figure 1.3. Purposes of documentation.

Purpose of Documenting	Use of the Documentation	How Documentation Is Collected	Types of Documentation	Status of Documentation	Documentation Shared With
Guide Instruction	To assist responding, planning next experiences, selecting materials	Ongoing with immediate reflection by educator	Work samples, observations and observational notes, notes from staff discussions, digital photographs	Raw, unprocessed	Colleagues, sometimes individual parents
Assessment	To document knowledge, skills, and dispositions of individual children for assessment	Ongoing; linked to curriculum goals and standards; may be formative or summative assessment	Work samples collected into portfolios, observations, photographic and video recordings	Raw, collected and summarized; rubrics may be applied	Parents and administration
Study Pedagogy	To provide insight into the teaching and learning process; for teacher training and professional growth; for professional learning communities	Ongoing; reflection is usually after the experience	Work samples, photographic and video recordings, transcribed tapes, anecdotal notes, staff dialogue notes, teacher journals	Raw; processed for discussion; published for sharing outside of immediate community	Colleagues, parents, professional learning communities, and professionals outside of the school
Communicate with Others	To communicate with others about what is happening in education programs	Ongoing collection; reviewed and selected for sharing based on communication goals	Selected work samples, photographic and video recordings, portions of transcribed tapes, notes, dialogues. All types of documentation can be shared	Processed and published with careful attention to good communication strategies; professional appearance and image	Parents, other professionals and the community

collected and with whom the documentation is shared. Documentation is an integral part of the education process, and the use of documentation for the purposes of guiding instruction, assessing learning, and studying pedagogy has been studied and written about extensively elsewhere (Cadwell, 1997, 2003; Edwards, Gandini, & Forman, 1998; Forman, 1996; Gandini, Hill, Cadwell, & Schwall, 2005; Helm, Beneke, & Steinheimer, 1998a & b; Katz & Chard, 1989). In this book, we focus on the processing and publishing of documentation for communication purposes.

Schools of Reggio Emilia

One source of interest in documentation, especially in early childhood programs, has come from the preschools of Reggio Emilia, Italy, where documentation is used extensively for studying pedagogy and guiding instruction. Through documentation of children's projects, however, the educators have also drawn public attention to the high-quality educational experience that occurs in their schools. They have been extremely successful in demonstrating, through documentation, the wealth of knowledge and skills gained by children in their programs. The documentation became especially useful for communication when, in the words of Lorus Malaguzzi (1998), "the need to make ourselves known became so strong" that the schools began sharing it in the community (p. 44).

Through a deliberate process of bringing the work of the children out into the community, sharing outcomes and teacher reflections throughout their town, they were able to develop respect for the schools and the staff. Eventually, this communication and advocacy effort led to financing of public preschools through city budget allocations. In addition, an exhibit of documentation of children's work, "The Hundred Languages of Children," has been displayed throughout the world, building the image of the schools internationally.

MEETING THE COMMUNICATION CHALLENGE FOR SCHOOLS TODAY

The challenges for schools that exist today require that educators communicate what is happening in their classrooms in clear and authentic ways. We can think about communication as a way to open windows for the community and decision makers such as legislators and school board members. As research continues to accumulate about the value of active, engaged, meaningful learning experiences for the development of intellect, the need to explain and demonstrate the value of these experiences increases. At the same time, there is research in communication fields about how to get ideas across, how to build credibility, and how to capture and hold attention. Professional communicators know that research and how to use it.

With this book we want to open windows for educators into the world of communication. We want to bring to teachers and school administrators the knowledge and skills that are so relevant and badly needed for the communication challenges that educators face today. We intend to show how educators can effectively use documentation (evidence of student learning) to open windows for others into the world of education.

Some readers may be tempted to jump to specific strategies in Part II or even to skip the strategies and jump to Part III for immediate ideas. We warn that to do that would be to miss the whole point of the book. To use documentation effectively, you must choose the strategies and the student work you share based on your audience. You must take the time to comprehend the needs and perceptions of the parents, families, and communities that you serve.

IN CHAPTER 2, YOU WILL LEARN about the unique challenges faced by today's educators and how becoming strategic in your communications will enable you to meet these challenges.

Opening Windows for Educators: The Need to Communicate Strategically

IN SPITE OF THE TREMENDOUS POWER of communication, most people usually communicate without being aware of the communication process. They write notes, post signs, create displays, and chat with others without planning or considering the communication process. They don't consciously consider audience needs or language issues. Without thinking, people, including educators, create messages intended to accomplish specific goals. They may even customize messages for different audiences. For example, a teacher will automatically use different terminology to tell fellow teachers about a math game than he would use to introduce the game to his 1st-grade class. Most of the time, we are able to exchange meanings successfully without thinking about the communication process, and we are satisfied with this. After the 1st-grade teacher's explanation, his colleagues probably understand how the game works and what learning objectives it might help students achieve. Likewise, after he introduces the game to his students, they probably understand how to play.

Yet communication, if designed to be as effective as possible, could potentially achieve far more than a simple exchange of messages. For example, a good teacher might not simply convey the game directions to students. Through word choice, expression, and organization, he could also communicate a number of other messages—that the game will be fun, that the skills used in the game are important, that the directions should be followed carefully. The teacher is not simply informing students how to play the game; he is also motivating the students to pay attention and be enthusiastic. Thus, while the teacher's primary goal is informative, he is also persuading at some level. If a teacher simply conveyed facts or directions, without motivating, captivating, and inspiring, most people would say that teacher was missing an opportunity to get more out of students.

How often are similar opportunities missed with other school audiences? Consider a letter sent home seeking permission for a student to participate in an upcoming field trip to the post office. With the communication process left on automatic, the teacher would most likely see this as an informative note with one obvious goal: getting the parents to return the required permission slip on time. But is that really all the teacher would like to achieve? Could the teacher use this communication opportunity to achieve more? If the teacher used this communication opportunity as a window to show the learning happening in her classroom, imagine what results could be achieved. If the parents understood the purpose of the trip, they could also extend the benefits. An inspired mother might encourage her daughter's excitement and get her to develop questions about the post office before the trip. An excited father might have the child tell what she saw after the trip to the post office, enhancing his daughter's memory of the trip, building her language skills as she tells the story, and building her confidence as the parent indicates that the trip is important. But the influence of these parents doesn't stop with their own child's experience of the field trip. Wouldn't it be nice if the teacher could be confident that not one parent thought the field trip detracted from the children's study of the "three R's"? Wouldn't it be nice if parents saw the trip as such a valuable learning experience that they later raised funds for more trips? These are just a few of the goals a teacher might achieve by strategically planning the field trip note.

With the communication process left on automatic, many people settle for a simple exchange of meanings when they could also inspire or persuade. Truly effective communication does not happen by accident. Professional communicators, such as advertisers, public relations practitioners, journalists, and speechwriters, take the communication process off automatic. They study the needs of each audience they must reach and consciously design messages to meet those needs and to persuade or inspire the audience to respond.

TODAY'S COMMUNICATION ENVIRONMENT

We may have reached a time when schools and teachers can no longer afford to leave their professional communication on automatic. Even though educators successfully exchange messages all the time while leaving the communication process on automatic, there are times when a simple exchange of messages is no longer sufficient for schools, even in communication with parents. Even a mere exchange of information is possible *only if* the audience is listening. As discussed in Chapter 1, social and political changes make it increasingly important for schools to reach out to audiences beyond students and parents. There are more ways to send messages—satellite, fax, Internet, e-mail, cell phones, answering machines, to name a few. The messages are transmitted faster, but there are also more of them. The same advances have changed the way people communicate, making it increasingly difficult to get messages through to people. Two specific changes in today's communication environment contribute to an increasingly urgent need for school professionals to look at the techniques of professional communicators:

- The increasing need to compete for an audience's attention
- The increasing expectations for professional-quality communication

Competition for an Audience's Attention

Simply getting people's attention has become more difficult. All audiences, including students and parents, have more information competing for their attention than ever before. Media outlets have multiplied and fragmented, with more magazines, radio stations, network television and cable channels. The Internet has added a totally new set of media options. In fact, industry statistics indicate the average person spends about 59% of his or her waking hours using online, print, audio, or video media (Biagi, 2000). Every day, most people are bombarded by hundreds of communications through regular mail, e-mail, and voicemail. The sheer quantity of informative and persuasive messages implies that audiences' attention will be distracted from the messages about their local schools. Furthermore, evidence suggests people are overwhelmed by information and respond by paying less attention to any of it, a reaction some professional communicators and scholars call information overload (Malhotra, 1982). In response to the proliferation of information, people have changed the way they receive communications. Most people tend to constantly scan their environment for relevant messages and then try to absorb only as much information as necessary without devoting much time to doing so. Only a few messages are selected for in-depth processing.

Increasing Expectations for Professional-Quality Communication

The number of professional communicators has multiplied along with the number of media outlets as America has entered the information age. The advertising industry alone employs 426,880 people in the United States, with professional communicators working for companies in all other industries as well and growth predicted for most communication-related professions (Bureau of Labor Statistics, 2004). Advertising and public relations messages, as well as news articles, television programs, and films, must be increasingly well crafted in order to break through the clutter, which means those industries have expanded and grown more sophisticated. In their desperation to stand out from the crowd, marketers increase their efforts to customize messages with personalized direct mail and telephone calls. Technological improvements continue to make it cheaper and easier to produce slick publications and striking visual effects.

Rising expectations for quality production reach far beyond Hollywood. Desktop publishing has become so widespread that in-home businesses can conveniently produce full-color brochures and families can announce their reunions in three-column newsletters—tasks that would have been difficult and expensive just 10 to 20 years ago. This means not only that school-related messages are aimed at an increasingly skeptical and harried audience already facing a sea of other messages but also that those other messages are often strikingly produced and professionally crafted.

THE NEED FOR TRAINED COMMUNICATORS IN SCHOOLS

Schools and other educational institutions habitually lag behind businesses in the number of personnel with knowledge and skills in communications. Nonprofit organizations, including schools, face an even more complex communication challenge than most businesses. Whereas businesses usually have one primary audience—customers—nonprofits usually have at least two primary audiences—one using the service and one funding it. For example, the Special Olympics would need ads encouraging participation and ads seeking donations and volunteers. These ads probably would not have the same audience or strategy. Major nonprofit organizations are rising to that challenge with an increasing investment in public relations. For example, Truman State University in Kirksville, Missouri, with 6,000 students, employs about 25 professional communicators in six departments: admissions, alumni relations, public affairs, public relations, sports information, and graphic arts. Yet school districts serving 20,000 students will sometimes have only one professionally trained communications staff member.

The communication environment public schools face is especially challenging—more than most businesses and even many nonprofits. Public schools, like other nonprofits, must rely in part on unselfish donations from people who do not directly receive anything in return—always a persuasive challenge! But unlike most nonprofits, public schools are also funded by involuntary donations through taxes. Some taxpayers who fund public schools do so with a negative attitude, and even some children and parents may be involved with public schools only because of legal requirements. Public schools are run by a citizen board whose members sometimes have little knowledge of education and may also have conflicting personal goals, yet those school boards usually have complete control over school finances and major decisions. The service that schools deliver—education—is closely tied to our society's values, which means emotions run high and opinions can be difficult to change.

Furthermore, the school's mission isn't to satisfy customers by giving them what they want. The school is charged with the difficult task of deciding what its customers need and convincing them that they want it. The gratification associated with the "product" is far from immediate. Students most directly receive the "product," and they may not even want to be there! The real decision makers, especially at the lower grade levels, are the parents, who only experience the product indirectly. To top it all off, the biggest source of information most parents have about what's going on at school is their children. Even the most honest 7-year-old may not accurately represent the teacher's work in the classroom! These challenges would give even a seasoned public relations team a headache. Private schools affiliated with religious organizations may face a different communication challenge—the organization and the school may have differing goals or expectations, and members of each may have different needs.

In spite of this challenging communication environment, grade schools and high schools may share one or two professional public relations representatives for a whole district, or even employ no professionally trained communicators at all. Communication with the many key audiences that affect schools often ends up being handled by already-busy principals, teachers, librarians, and music directors.

Frequently, these professional educators have little, if any, communication training. They are not alone. With increasing expectations for professional-quality writing and production, people in many industries across many levels of responsibility find they are expected to communicate professionally without the knowledge and skills to do so.

BECOMING PROFESSIONAL ABOUT COMMUNICATION

We do not intend to add to the heavy workload of dedicated educators by asking them to assume the role of public relations executives for their schools. However, it is clear from our observations of schools that many of the challenges and difficulties that schools are facing today could be lessened if schools were better at telling their story. By developing the habit of communicating strategically, teachers and school staff have the opportunity to persuade and inspire their audiences and build relationships. Contemplating the potential power of strategic communication may very well inspire teachers to seek out new, additional communication opportunities, such as a classroom newsletter. Our main goal, however, is to change the way that educators already communicate with their myriad audiences, to help them think strategically about the messages they are already communicating, in order to tap the persuasive potential of those communication opportunities. This book does not necessarily call on educators to communicate more often, but rather to communicate more effectively.

In some respects, teachers are already professional communicators. In order to teach, teachers must communicate with their students. Teachers have spent years studying the characteristics of the children they teach. They have carefully cultivated habits of effective teaching, including adapting language and concepts to the children's level, presenting appropriate quantities of information, showing how material is relevant, inspiring enthusiasm, and capturing and holding students' attention. This does not happen by accident. It happens because a teacher has developed a skill of conveying enthusiasm or because a teacher has planned a lesson in advance based on what he or she knows about the students. Thus, teachers are already in the habit of communicating strategically. However, these strategies are often limited to a very specific audience (their students) in a specific communication situation (the classroom).

Professional communicators study not only one particular audience but also communication strategies that can be adapted for all audiences and situations. What really distinguishes professional communicators is that they take the communication process off automatic and use it intentionally. Their strategies can be valuable for educators as they communicate with school audiences, such as parents, co-workers, principals, school boards, and partner businesses. This book draws from the disciplines professional communicators study—communications, public relations, design, and even museumology—to give teachers, principals, and other school staff the basics they need to make the most of communication opportunities. We place particular emphasis on the tremendous communication opportunity provided by the documentation of engaged learning methods.

DEFINING STRATEGIC COMMUNICATION

One of the ways that professional communicators accomplish their goals is to communicate *strategically*. In strategic communication, the communicator consciously recognizes communication goals and consciously designs the message to increase the likelihood of achieving those goals, including goals not explicitly stated in the message. Only by strategically designing communication can an individual hope to take full advantage of a communication opportunity.

Persuasive communication is a type of communication that educators use naturally. Persuasive communication can be defined as communication with the goal of changing a person's attitude or behavior. Many simple messages meet this definition of persuasive communication. A "wet paint" sign informs the reader without providing any explicit directions about the writer's desired effect, but the writer does have a goal. The communication is shorthand: The reader knows the real message is "don't touch this wall," and the reader is probably fully persuaded not to touch it! Likewise, even the flattest and most uninspiring field trip permission note could be described as a persuasive message. If the parent returns the signed slip, the desired effect is achieved. But these messages are not strategic.

Strategic communication goes beyond persuasive communication to conscious consideration of the audience and communication goals. In strategic communication, the communicator consciously recognizes communication goals and consciously designs the persuasive message to increase the likelihood of achieving those goals, including goals not explicitly stated in the message. Only by strategically designing communication can an individual hope to take full advantage of a communication opportunity.

In some messages, such as national television commercials, every word has been strategically chosen for its likely effect on the audience, and the effects of different words, gestures, and music were actually tested on sample audiences. This may work for 30-second commercials representing investments of several million dollars and even higher potential profits, but certainly it would not be practical for all messages! Even professional communicators cannot always afford this kind of care. A journalist on a deadline or a company spokesperson responding to questions in a crisis cannot take time to carefully consider every word, but they can still be more effective than the average person might be in the same situation. Communication does not have to be a work of art to be strategic and effective. Professional communicators are often able to communicate strategically under very tight time pressures, and educator-communicators can adopt a few of these same techniques in order to design more effective communication without spending a lot more time.

Professional communicators have a toolbox of standard steps, such as analyzing the audience, selecting evidence, and adapting language, which they can do quickly and efficiently. These steps aren't a matter of spending hours crafting the perfect language in a note; these steps are a matter of thinking consciously (strategically!) about communication. Spending an extra minute reviewing the note to ask "Is this message communicating what I want?" can make a difference. In Part II, Strategies for Becoming Educator-Communicators, we will explain some of those key building tools by describing them as strategies that can be adapted by schools, centers, and education agencies; we also show how they can be used for school audiences.

Professional communicators also develop shortcuts for specific projects. For example, a journalist might have a standard paragraph he uses to explain a complicated tax issue to citizens, or a lobbyist might have a file of statistics and anecdotes she can use to support her cause. Chapter 11, Foundation Builders, tells how to develop such files. Other tools they use are templates or patterns for certain communications or systems to follow to assemble a communication. Some of these are included in Chapter 12, Tools for Opening Windows.

HOWEVER, SHORTCUTS AND TEMPLATES will not help educator-communicators unless they know how to be strategic. That begins with understanding the communication process outlined in Chapter 3.

PART II

Strategies for Becoming Educator-Communicators

Window on the Communication Process: How Professional Communicators View Communication

One way to take the communication process off automatic and make it strategic is to take a few moments to step back and look at the process. Of course, teachers and principals do not have time to do a theoretical analysis every time they communicate! Neither do journalists on deadline or public relations practitioners in a crisis. Yet professional communicators' basic understanding of the communication process helps shape their habit of effective strategic communication and suggests many practical strategies to communicate accurately and effectively. This chapter presents an overview of a basic model of communication. The other chapters in this part discuss how educators can apply professional communicators' strategies to make each piece of the process as effective as possible.

THE COMMUNICATION PROCESS

Communication scholars view communication in terms of transmission—transmitting an idea from one person to another. Figure 3.1 summarizes professional communicators' view of the communication process. Many communication scholars have proposed countless versions of the communication model, but David Berlo (1960) can be credited with outlining the four basic elements: *sender*, *receiver*, *message*, and *channel*. This diagram of the communication model shows a one-way process, but it is important to keep in mind that the process is circular—the speaker sends the message to the listener, but then the listener becomes the speaker and the process is repeated.

Accurate communication means the receiver's idea is close to the one the sender had in mind. Most of us have at one time or another had the experience of playing a game similar to Gossip. A message is sent by one person at the beginning of a line of people to the person at the end of the line by whispering it to the next person, who whispers it to the next, who in turn whispers it to the next. It is always a surprise when the message arriving at the receiver at the end of the line differs from the message first sent at the beginning of the line. In daily communication experiences, it doesn't take a long line of communications for the message of the sender to be misunderstood. Effective communication means the receiver not only accurately receives the message sent but also responds to the message as the sender hoped. Documentation of children's work, introduced in Chapter 1, has much potential as a tool for communicating both accurately and effectively about children's learning.

Encoding

The communication process begins when the communicator, or sender, has an idea he or she wants to share. The sender captures this idea in a message, some form the audience or "receiver" can sense—hear, read, see, smell, taste, or touch. Typically, the sender puts the idea into spoken or written words and pictures, but other senses can be part of the message, too. For example, when a parent says to a child, "See how soft the

Figure 3.1. The communication process.

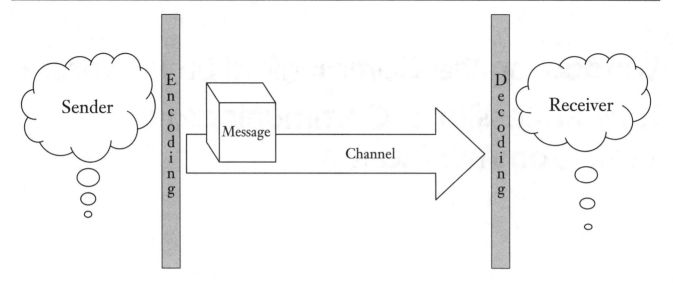

kitten's fur feels," and presents the kitten for the child to pet, the kitten and the touch of its soft fur are part of the message. This process of packaging the idea into a message is called encoding. It is this encoded message that is sent to the receiver, not the original idea. It is the thoughts that we are interested in sharing, but the sender and receiver can never see each other's thoughts directly, only through the filter of observable messages. Human language is amazingly sophisticated, but still everyone has experienced the struggle to find the right words to express an idea. The encoded message is never exactly the same as the original idea—what is said is not always what is meant, and not everything contained in the idea can be captured in the message.

We might picture the sender packing up the message, tying it with a bow, and dropping it in the mail to the receiver. However, if the sender does this without awareness or attention to the whole communication process or an understanding of the culture of the receiver, what is unwrapped may be disappointing to both the giver and receiver.

In fact, symbols and codes often jump into the package with the message and become part of it, intentionally or not! For example, misspellings in a teacher's letter to parents convey a lack of professionalism. Other codes could be nonverbal behavior that expresses the sender's unconscious attitudes, the relationship between the sender and receiver, the sender's natural communication style, the situation, or even simply who the sender is. The receiver will use those other symbols and codes, or *subtext*, to draw conclusions about the sender's intentions,

motivation, and believability. Those conclusions influence the receiver's understanding of the message and his or her response. Recognizing these codes and managing the subtext is part of strategic communication. Strategy Two, "Invest in the Most Credible Communicators: Teachers, Principals, and Children," will discuss one important aspect of this subtext, credibility.

Channel

The way the message is delivered is the channel. The channel could be simply speaking directly to someone, but more often communication professionals are interested in more formal channels such as a presentation, a display, or the mass media, including television and newspaper. Each channel has its own characteristics and expectations that shape how the message can be encoded and sent and how the audience receives the message. For example, radio is a purely audio channel—it is simply not possible to include any kind of visual information. Instead, the sender must use language and sounds to help the listener imagine a picture. Likewise, the size of a school display board limits how much information can be conveyed through that channel. The characteristics of each channel represent limitations and opportunities for making communication effective.

Decoding

Once the audience receives the message, it must be decoded into an idea. Just as the sender's knowledge, attitudes, and life experiences influence the encoding process, the receiver's knowledge, attitudes, and life experiences influence the decoding process. Words, pictures, sounds, and all forms of packaging a message can mean different things to different people.

The encoding and decoding processes might be seen as filters. Each person filters the message through his or her own vocabulary and experiences. The sender's and receiver's shared cultural experience includes knowledge of a great many codes. Language is an easily understood code; however, it is not the only shared code. A business card and suit are widely recognized as codes for professionalism; making eye contact signifies sincerity; nodding and listening while tilting one's head say "I'm listening"; and tone of voice often conveys enthusiasm. However, the picture is more complex than it might initially seem. For example, making eye contact does not signify sincerity in all cultures, and a body movement that might suggest enthusiasm in one culture might be interpreted as boastfulness in another.

The receiver is far from being an empty vessel waiting for the message. The receiver not only interprets signals sent unintentionally, but also seeks out signals and draws conclusions even when the sender does nothing. Messages are sent all the time, not just when the sender wants to send one—a teacher who talks only to her native-English-speaking parents at an open house has sent a message to the Hispanic parents just as surely as she has sent messages to the English-speakers; a school that does not share positive evidence of children's progress with the taxpayers has communicated just as surely as the state office that distributed the test score report to the media. Understanding the receiver's needs, interests, and background helps make strategic communication efforts more effective; audience analysis will be discussed in Strategy One.

ADAPTING THE COMMUNICATION PROCESS FOR EDUCATORS

The strategic use of documentation is a way to ensure that the message that schools and centers send is both accurate and effective. The collection and sharing of evidence of student learning is both a wonderful *gift* to share with parents and the community and also the *gift wrap* and bow for a variety of important messages in education! In Figure 3.2 documentation is added to the communication process, and the communication process is adapted to the educational setting.

- The senders in this model are trained, credible educator-communicators.
- The message now provides evidence of student learning.
- The channels are now the primary channels used by schools and institutions serving children, including newsletters, community displays, school bulletin boards, websites, and press releases for local media.
- The receivers are now the stakeholders in the

Figure 3.2. Using documentation as a communication strategy.

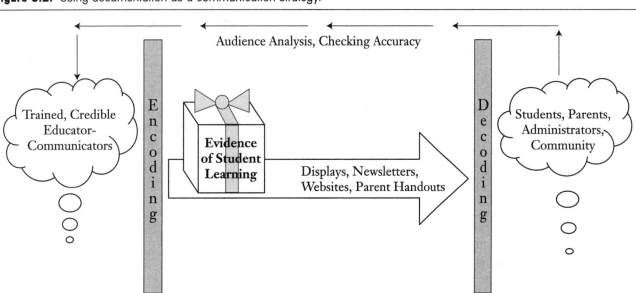

educational process—children, parents, administrators, and members of the community.
- Added to the communication diagram is a clear feedback loop in which the credible communicators are consistently listening to and analyzing the needs of the audience.

Once the communication process is understood, educator-communicators can begin to think strategically. The next chapters present seven strategies that educators can use to improve the communication process for their schools, programs, and communities. These strategies, which are based on knowledge, skills, and research from professional communicators, are the following:

- *Strategy One.* Analyze your audience: Understanding education audiences
- *Strategy Two.* Invest in the most credible communicators: Teachers, principals, and children
- *Strategy Three.* Convince with evidence: The power of documentation
- *Strategy Four.* Plan your message: Deciding what to say
- *Strategy Five.* Incorporate evidence: Ways to share your documentation
- *Strategy Six.* Follow design conventions: Making communication look professional
- *Strategy Seven.* Reach out to the media: Connecting with your community

CHAPTER 4

Strategy 1

Analyze Your Audience: Understanding Education Audiences

WHEN PLANNING COMMUNICATION, professional communicators often use the audience as a starting point, working backwards through the communication model. They begin by deciding who the audiences are and analyzing the needs of those audiences. By knowing these needs, they can better serve these audiences and decide what relationships they wish to establish and what messages they wish to communicate or what relationships should be established.

This purposeful analysis of audiences may not sit well with some education professionals who see this function of professional communicators as manipulative, activating images of advertisers and slick public relations campaigns. In reality, marketing is consumer-centered. It is oriented toward identifying needs, designing products and services that meet these needs, and promoting those products and services so they are accessible. The negative connotation of marketing comes from the idea that marketing is sometimes used to "sell" or "push" items on people, encouraging them to perceive as needs items or ideas that society might question. Education, however, is a legitimate need recognized by society, and educator-communicators provide information audiences want and need to know. Using professional communication strategies enables educational institutions to more effectively meet that need.

Analyzing education audiences in many cases will involve using data on parents and communities already being gathered and used for school improvement. Knowing audience needs enables the educational institution to meet the needs of that audience. This information also makes it possible to package communication messages so they can be most effective—but it's not just about that gift wrap and bow; it's about choosing a gift that will be useful and appreciated. Truly effective communication is a gift from the sender to the receiver. The receiver comes away with something valuable—knowledge, understanding, a new perspective, inspiration to act—he or she did not have before.

Public relations practitioners often start by identifying stakeholders. Stakeholders include anyone who has a stake, an investment or involvement, in an organization—anyone who is affected by the organization or affects the organization. Who are the stakeholders in education? Most of society is interested in the care and education of its children. Our preschools, childcare centers, afterschool care programs, and schools contribute significantly to the shaping of our future taxpayers, business leaders, politicians, labor force, voters, activists, and artists. Many groups can be seen as stakeholders in the education process. Students and parents are the most significant partners.

Stakeholders may also be audiences for each other in the education process. Principals or center directors are another key audience for teachers, while teachers are a key audience for principals and center directors.

Schools and centers often have another key audience with significant power over the school but relatively indirect involvement—a school board, advisory board, or the board of a supporting organization such as a church, synagogue, or agency.

In an ideal world, a school public relations staff would follow the pattern of other public relations professionals, identifying key stakeholder groups and developing a long-range, proactive, strategic communication plan for each, sharing that plan with the most credible communicators in the educational institution. However, we all know that this is not an ideal world. School public relations offices may be greatly understaffed or even nonexistent; center directors and principals may be squeezing public relations in among myriad other activities. But individual teachers, principals, center directors, and other staff are already communicating regularly with many audiences, and a little audience analysis can go a long way toward making this communication more effective. Taking an hour or even a half-hour one time each year or one time each semester for focused reflection on who key audiences are, what they need, and how communication could be designed to meet those needs can increase the effectiveness of communications throughout the year. This chapter presents the basics of audience analysis, with an emphasis on how it applies to what is probably the most important school audience (other than the students!)—parents. Then ways to adapt analysis for other audiences are presented.

AUDIENCE ANALYSIS: FOCUS ON PARENTS

Communication and marketing professionals usually look at four types of information when they try to analyze or define an audience: *demographics, psychographics, benefits,* and *usage*. Ideally, teachers and principals would take time at the beginning of each year to think carefully about who the parents of their students are, with a particular focus on how this might impact communications. Building a detailed description of the audience helps a communicator think about what information the audience needs and how that audience decodes or interprets messages. Chapter 11, Foundation Builders, provides worksheets you can use to guide you through each category of analysis.

Demographics

Demographics refers to *observable facts* about the audience: age, marital status, income, educational level, ethnic background, number of children in the family, ages of children in the family, family structure, and job status. The primary language spoken at home may also be part of this information. At first glance, demo-graphics may seem dry, but looking at these simple facts can tell a communicator a lot about what kind of language is appropriate for this audience and what their concerns might be. Marketers and public relations professionals often start with demographics simply because this is the information they have access to. This is equally true for schools and childcare centers. Demographic information is on file as part of school or childcare center records.

A good starting point for audience analysis is to describe the demographic characteristics and then look at each characteristic and consider how it might impact the way the audience interprets your messages. If the parents of your students are very diverse, it may be hard to write a demographic description. One approach is to look for segments: Can you group parents into two or three "categories" using the data that you have? For example, if you have data on your parents by zip code, you could group them by zip code. Do you have income data? This could be another category. In some cases a category will not affect communication. Zip code, for instance, might have no significance for communication for a childcare center where children are dropped off on the way to work. However, categories by zip code may be extremely helpful for a community arts program. Describe each category, and consider how communications can be designed to reach all of them.

It is a good idea to actually review the files and formally gather information for a demographic analysis of the audience and to periodically repeat this process. Communicators (amateurs and professionals alike) may think they know the demographics of the key audience off the top of their heads, but this is really just their perception of that audience. It is easy to see an audience as we wish it to be, or to imagine the whole audience to be like the people we have gotten to know best, or not to realize that demographics are changing for our group. A director of a childcare center may think that his children are from two-parent families, but this picture may not be accurate. A new teacher may presume the parents will be much like the parents of the school she taught in before. Socioeconomic levels of school districts and neighborhoods may shift over time, making once-accurate perceptions of an audience outdated.

Although most public schools routinely gather these data, other educational organizations, especially small community organizations, may not have such data. If you are associated with these organizations, you will want to think about what data would be helpful to gather and how to collect it. You may be able to compile information you already know from working with the families. If you are providing services to children, schools will often share data with you, and data are available for the communities and neighborhoods. Libraries and agencies such as United Way can be helpful.

The first step in the demographic analysis is building a description. The second step is considering the implications for communication. Most schools and centers already gather this information and review it for lesson planning and projecting class size, staffing needs, transportation needs, and other decision making. In fact, that director may well know exactly what percentage of children in the center come from single-parent homes but still communicate as if most of the families resemble the Cleavers. The center director and new teacher in the example above could potentially improve their effectiveness by taking some time at the beginning of the school year to look at the demographic description with a specific focus on communication implications. One approach might be to make a list of communication guidelines based on those implications. For example, the center director might conclude that newsletters and invitations to school events should not use language such as "parents" but instead should use more flexible and inclusive language so families with other structures do not feel alienated. Additionally, she might note that many of the children are being raised by grandparents or that grandparents play a major role in the children's lives. This process has benefits beyond merely using inclusive language to view grandparents as an important audience and consider their needs. For example, if grandparents are older, maybe it would be helpful to ensure that adult seating is provided in classrooms at open house type events. (New or expectant moms might appreciate the extra chairs, too!) Perhaps it would be helpful to give parents an opportunity to ask that grandparents be included in invitation mailings and volunteer requests even if they are not official guardians.

As they prepare for a new school year, educators spend time reviewing files that include demographic information and considering implications for the educational process. Audience analysis, in which the same information is simply viewed with an eye for implications for the communication process, could simply be incorporated into that usual procedure. To link raw demographic facts to communication implications, it may help to consider three questions in light of this information:

- What are the strengths of the current communication approach for reaching these groups?
- What are the weaknesses of the current communication approach?
- What specific changes could be realistically made to better reach the audience this year or this semester?

Figure 4.1 shows how a teacher in a dual-language kindergarten might analyze the demographics of her parent audience, using the worksheet provided in Chapter 11, Foundation Builders. The dual-language emphasis of the program and the two languages spoken at home have implications for all communications.

Psychographics

Psychographics refers to psychological or lifestyle characteristics of the audience: their values and attitudes. These are not clearly measurable facts, and schools and centers may not have this information conveniently at hand. Consider for example:

- What issues are most important for parents of your students?
- What do you know about their religion?
- How do they spend their leisure time?
- Do they have a strong identification with their ethnic background?
- Are they sports enthusiasts?
- Are they art aficionados?

Note that ethnicity is listed under demographics, but ethnic identification is also a psychographic. Knowing that many parents are Asian American does not tell the full story: Is that a strong part of their identity or simply a genealogical heritage? What values are parts of that heritage? Are they actively involved in an ethnic community?

Likewise, educational level of the parents is a demographic, but the value placed on education is a psychographic characteristic. Imagine that most parents have significantly less or more education than the teacher. That information alone can be useful for deciding what kind of language to use in displays and letters home, but it does not tell the whole story. You should also try to find out the following:

Do the parents place a high value on education? Do they respect schools?

Figure 4.1. Example of demographic analysis—Public school.

Demographic	Most of My Families	Some of My Families	Communication Implications
Educational Level, Socioeconomic	One in five families have a college degree; some have low literacy Blue collar 38% on reduced lunch		• Use low-literacy style for notes • Telephone • Be sensitive about $$
Language	52% Spanish-speakers	48% English-speakers	Translate *everything*
Ethnic Background	Hispanic	White	
Ages of Parents	Parents generally in late 20s ; not sure if any were teen parents		
Age Groups of Children in Home *Ex: Infant/Toddlers, Preschoolers, Elementary Age, High School*	≈ Three children with 2–4 years separation; older siblings and cousins translate	≈ 1 or 2 children with 2–4 years separation	Provide free child care for events; include in all notices that child care is available
Family Structure *Ex: Married, Single Parent, Grandparents*	Mostly two-parent homes, ≈ one in five single parents. Grandparents help out after school		Chat with grandmas when they pick up children; include them in efforts to read at home, etc.
Job Schedules *Ex: Two Parents Working, Part-Time Working*	Mom and Dad work different shifts; several work night shifts		Evening meetings hard to avoid, but switch night of week

Do they long for their children to have educational opportunities they never had?

Are they suspicious of the value of academic learning and uncomfortable in the school environment?

Are they highly educated and determined that their children enter the best universities and become highly educated also?

Psychographic information is not easy to obtain. Information can be gathered from parent surveys after children enter a program. Asking questions such as "Can you tell us your dreams for your child? What do you hope he or she will be like at 21?" can be fun and very insightful. This question was asked of parents of preschoolers at the Valeska Hinton Early Childhood Education Center in Peoria, Illinois. Many of the answers included a desire that their children be independent, drug- and alcohol-free, and happy. This gave the staff an idea of the importance of these issues to many of the families. The staff was then able to help parents understand how the preschool curriculum contributed to those long-term goals by fostering independence

and self-confidence. Questions such as "Do you celebrate religious or ethnic holidays and which you would like us to know about?" or "What family activities does your child especially enjoy?" provide insight into both the child and the family. Informal conversations also provide a lot of this information.

Anything you know about the families you work with and the culture and reference groups to which they belong can help you understand their values and concerns. Resource books about working with families of other cultures often discuss key psychographic issues. For example, many teachers have found the book *Framework for Understanding Poverty* (Payne, 2005) to be helpful for better understanding of, and therefore better communication with, their children and families.

As with demographics, describing the audience is only the first step. The next step is to consider how these characteristics impact the way the audience decodes or interprets messages and how messages might be better designed for them. For example, imagine how two groups of parents might respond to a parent orientation explaining the Project Approach teaching method. One group is less educated and negative about schooling, while the other group is less educated but still positive about schooling. Even if the teacher does a good job of putting concepts into plain language they can understand, the parents may interpret or decode the message differently based on their values and attitudes toward schooling. If the explanation emphasized research and expert opinions, the first group might feel alienated and skeptical, but the second group might be impressed and excited. For the first group, a more powerful approach might be to focus instead on how the Project Approach draws on children's everyday experiences and builds practical skills for lifelong learning. If the audience includes both groups of parents, the teacher would be wise to focus on both aspects of the benefits of the approach rather than one aspect only.

The analysis of psychographics in Figure 4.2 is for a church preschool program. The families who attend this preschool highly value academic achievement. Although most of the parents are very involved with their children, some are extremely busy with their careers and do not spend much time with their children. This is the kind of information that can come from a psychographic analysis. It is especially helpful information to a program that has values or lifestyles as part of its teaching goals, as this Christian program does.

The next two types of analysis involve thinking about how parents (or other audiences) view the school or center.

Benefits to Audience

You should also focus on the benefits the audience gets out of the school, educational program, or child-care center:

Figure 4.2. Example of psychographic analysis—Church preschool.

Psychographic	Most of My Families	Some of My Families	Communication Implications
Identification with Ethnicity	Have minimal identification with ethnic background; live in diverse neighborhoods.	Strong ethnic, cultural identification; in United States temporarily with business.	Parents with strong ethnic/cultural background need to feel welcome. Orientation to customs and procedures of preschool.
Lifestyle *Ex: Time Spent with Family*	About half of children have stay-at-home mom, busy social lives, include children in many activities.	Have live-in nanny for child care ; parents travel often on business; children and parents are often separated.	Nannies and other caregivers included in parent get-togethers during the day; information on child rearing; communications to parents by most convenient method (e-mail?, web access?).
Religion	Three-fourths of parents are Christian and came to school for the Christian education component.	A few parents are not practicing members of any faith group.	Should explanations of faith practices be included in communications? Invitations to faith groups?
Values *Ex: Sports,* *Music,* *Participation in Community*	Sports participation by parents and children is strong—soccer, softball, jogging, biking; reading and education valued.	A few parents place highest priority on academic achievement and performance.	Show academic value of engaged learning experiences; Show value of looking at a variety of experiences for child and role of dispositions in contributing to success.
Other *Ex: Parent Participation in Child Rearing*	See role as being important; want to actively participate.	A few of our parents see role as providing high-quality preschool , caregivers, toys, and access to experts for children. Children and parents are scheduled into many activities.	Include in communications what parents and children can do together. Provide information on low-stress family activities in community in monthly calendar.

- *What do the parents expect the program to provide for their child?*
  Education?
  Stimulation?
  Broadening of horizons?
  Social interaction?
  Life skills?
  Discipline?
  Personal encouragement?
- *What about benefits directly for parents themselves?*
  Reassurance that the child is progressing normally?
  Parenting support and suggestions?
  A resource for social services?
  A babysitter?

Again, it may be very difficult to describe the whole group of parents. Professional marketers often analyze by segments, or use information about benefits different people want from a product to group people. For example, a computer firm using benefit segmentation might classify home-computer users into three groups: people who use the computer primarily for managing household business, people who use the computer mainly for photography and home video, and people who use the computer mainly for games. The same computer may work for each group, but each has different questions about buying a computer. Marketers try to understand the needs of each group and to customize the way they communicate with each group or design communications that will work for all three groups.

It may be helpful for teachers and principals to think about different benefit segments among parents. This is not about classifying people and treating them differently! This analytical process is about recognizing the different needs of different audience members and working to ensure that all communications—such as notes home, parent newsletters, field trip permissions, and parent conferences—meet the diverse needs of all the parent audiences.

For example, consider a kindergarten teacher getting ready for a new school year. Half of the children know many letters by name, can count to 10, and will be coming from a preschool experience; the other half will be entering school for the first time, knowing no letters and being unable to count. Most likely then, the parents of the latter children are primarily concerned about getting two benefits out of kindergarten for their children: learning to read and adjusting to the school environment. For other half, these benefits are not primary concerns. If the teacher focuses all his parent communications on letters, counting to 10, and

adjusting to school, half of the parents may tune out or, worse yet, presume their child is not getting much out of school since he or she has already achieved those goals. These parents are concerned about raising beginning reading to a higher level and building other skills. Recognizing that there are two key groups may help the teacher make sure that most communications have some information that is meaningful and important for each group. The kindergarten teacher already strategically designs classroom activities to meet the needs of both groups of children. He also needs to strategically design communications to parents to meet the needs of both groups.

Another way to look at benefits is to consider the need to inform an audience of the importance of a benefit that is not primary for that audience. For example, a director of an afterschool program may find that some parents see babysitting as the primary benefit, with giving children a break from the structured school environment perhaps as a secondary benefit. If the program philosophy includes providing a valuable learning experience for children, teachers and administrators will need to recognize that learning is not initially seen as a key benefit of the afterschool program, at least not for this particular parent audience. Communications with this audience will likely be ineffective if they simply try to persuade the audience that the children are learning. Part of the communication challenge will include persuading this parent audience that quality learning experiences and intellectual stimulation are benefits they should seek in an afterschool care program.

Usage

While benefits focus on outcomes gained, usage focuses on how the audience uses the school or childcare center, primarily on when and how often. This can be especially important for childcare centers or community education programs where usage may vary widely from family to family or program to program and can have a major impact on communication with that audience. Marketers often segment people into heavy, medium, and light users of a product. Consider how heavy, medium, and light "users" of a childcare center have different concerns and communication needs:

- How regularly do parents and children see the teacher or the classroom?
- Is the center a second home for the child or an occasional babysitter?

- What is missed when the child or parent is away, and does that need to be communicated?

Figure 4.3 shows a benefits and usage analysis for a community college childcare center.

While most schools have fairly regular "usage" patterns among students, contact with parents can vary widely. Some parents may drop their children off and pick them up daily, stopping to chat with the teacher and look at work displayed in the classroom, and may volunteer in the classroom on a regular basis. Others may come into school only a few times a year for a parent conference or open house. In order to be meaningful to both groups, communications will need to have fresh, engaging information that will be interesting to the highly involved parents but will also include background information so that less involved parents aren't confused. Feeling confused and uncomfortable will not encourage anyone to become more involved!

One tactic for minimizing confusion for "low-usage" groups is to always include basic information needed by less involved parents to successfully participate even if they have not participated previously.

For example, every newsletter should include contact information for the teacher. Every invitation to an evening or weekend parent event should include the room number and, if relevant, where to park and which door to enter. When formatting newsletters or invitations, this information can consistently appear in a box with a border. The box and the consistent format will signal to involved readers that they already know this information and can skip it. Another idea for communicating with low-usage audiences is to clearly tell what they can expect or what action you expect from them.

Another tactic to keep audiences with varying levels of interaction in the loop is to have optional background information on hand. For example, handouts on the program's teaching philosophy and portfolio assessment system should be available at every parent event. Once time has been invested in creating these background documents, you might as well get more use out of them. Those who want additional information can pick up the handout; but merely having it out does not waste time or detract in any way from the experience of those who already know that information.

Figure 4.3. Example of benefits and usage analysis—Community college childcare center.

	Most of My Families	Some of My Families	Implications for Communication
How much do they use the center?	Most of our families use the child-care center for child care while they attend classes at the community college—as little as 9 hours per week—time matching class schedule.	Use the child-care center for full-day care while the parents work at the community college. 40 hours/week. A few of the parents use the child-care center for an educational experience for the children—12 hours/week.	Most contact is part time. Commitment to center is low by child and parent when usage low. Communication needs to make them feel more a part of the center.
What do they see as the primary purpose of the center in their life?	Child care and part of the opportunity that they as adults have to get an education—a service of the college.	Child care provided as a benefit of working at the college. An educational experience for their child available because the college is in their community.	Emphasize the quality of care and the educational benefit of the center; use children's work and photos of the children in displays in college. Spotlight ongoing long-term experiences such as projects for children.
What do they see as benefits of choosing this center over others?	Convenience.	Convenience and quality Quality and educational experience for their child.	Emphasize professionalism of staff in all communications. Show child development majors working with children . Use standards and accreditation information in all brochures and signs.

Specific Communications: Benefits and Usage

Another useful way to look at benefits and usage from the audience perspective is to focus less on the benefits gained from and the usage of the school or program in general, and instead consider the benefits gained from and the usage of a particular communication, such as a newsletter, field trip permission slip, or parent night.

For example, a teacher planning a parent night needs to consider what benefits the parents will gain from the program:

- Information about the children's activities and progress?
- An opportunity to bond with the children and share their learning experience?
- An opportunity to build a relationship with the teacher?
- An understanding of the school's teaching methodology?

The teacher should also consider whether the benefits she hopes for are the same as the benefits the parents seek. How can the communication event be planned to maximize those benefits?

Usage should also be considered by the teacher:

- *How will parents and guardians "use" the parent night?*
  Will they come in and out?
  Will they stay for a formal program?
- *How much effort will the audience put into achieving the benefits?*
  Will they show up with a list of specific questions about the child's progress?
  Will they guide the child through giving them a tour of the project and classroom?
- *Will they be nervous and uncertain about what reaction their children are looking for?*

It might be most useful to think of usage of a specific communication from the reverse perspective: What are the obstacles to full usage of the parent night?

- Will they be distracted by trying to keep an eye on younger siblings? Perhaps childcare or activities for youngsters would help.
- How are they going to get there—should public transportation schedules be considered in planning?

- Will work schedules be an obstacle for attendance? What options or alternatives exist?
- Will the parent and guardian guests know what to do once they get there? Would it be helpful to provide suggestions for how to get the most out of the parent night or things to ask the children to show them? A classroom display can include questions, which often encourage parents to read them aloud to their children, or parents might be handed a card with "Ask your child to show you . . . ."

It may not always be clear whether audience characteristics or considerations fit under demographics, psychographics, benefits, or usage. It really does not matter. The value of this framework is providing a starting point to guide communicators through the process of building understanding of the audience. For key audiences, such as parents, it is well worth investing a little time in a focused analysis of each category of information and giving careful consideration to how communications could be adapted to reach those audiences.

ANALYZING OTHER AUDIENCES

The audience analysis process discussed above can be used for any communication audience. Educators, particularly center directors and principals, might consider identifying key stakeholders besides parents and doing an audience analysis for one or more of those as well. Some of these might include the following:

- Taxpayers
- Geographic neighbors
- Schools sending students to your program
- Schools receiving students from your program
- Agencies or organizations sharing students
- Sponsoring agencies (for nonpublic schools) and their advisory or governing boards
- Volunteers
- Corporate supporters or donators of services
- Legislators
- Accrediting or regulatory agencies
- School board members

Audience analyses need not be done on all these groups, nor do they need to be done all at the same time. The use of audience analysis is not limited to directors and principals. All educator-communicators can benefit from simply making an effort to consider the message and the presentation of that message from the audience's perspective, to walk in the audience's shoes. This is especially important when the communicator's and audience's shoes are quite different and common goals are less clear, such as when educators reach out to audiences beyond schools.

The benefits for outside audiences are complex, subtle, and often quite different from the benefits that interest the communicator. When dealing with parents and school audiences, shared interest in educating the children unites them in a common goal. This is less clear for outside audiences. Here we discuss the benefits for three key audiences: community members who do not have children in the schools, the business community, and other educators.

Community Members Without Children in the Schools

This audience can be important for several reasons. For a public school, these people are probably taxpayers. Few for-profit marketers find themselves in such a challenging situation: having an audience that is legally required to fund a service but receives no direct benefit, and providing indirect benefits that are revealed only many years later! Yet this group plays a major role in deciding how much funding public schools should have. Some private schools or centers may be associated with another organization (such as a church) whose members are in a similar situation—their money goes toward the school, but they have no direct control and realize few direct benefits.

The primary benefit these audiences receive is educated, contributing adults—the "product" of a quality education system. Thus, these audiences tend to be focused on results. For members of organizations that support a school or center, the key benefit may be related to the mission of the organization. For example, members of a religious group may sponsor a school so that they can help raise children with certain religious values; a company may sponsor a center in order to provide convenient, affordable, and quality child care for employees; an immigrant community may sponsor a school or center in order to keep cultural traditions alive. These benefits are of primary importance to these audiences, and communications need to demonstrate links to these benefits. For example, in communications with the supporting religious group, the school would incorporate the religious-values mission. In communications with a sponsoring company, a childcare center may want to emphasize parent (employee) benefits. One way to do this may be to add a mission-related panel or poster when a display goes in the hallway of the faith group or in the executive cafeteria at the firm. While communications may focus on academic learning, these other benefits should be included when the audience sees them as a primary benefit.

For these audiences, "usage" of the schools is extremely low. They may have little to no direct interaction with the school and probably receive few if any direct communications. This means they are distant from the day-to-day life of the schools. Some may prefer to keep it that way.

For example, community members who do not have children in the schools sometimes need to be persuaded to even pay attention to communications from schools. Reaching this audience is a major challenge because educators need to open windows into the learning process so this audience will recognize the needs of schools and centers; however, the audience may not be especially interested in looking into the window. It is not surprising that this audience is often interested in standardized assessment as a neat, efficient way to keep aware of achievement levels of schools so they can do their duty as voting citizens. They need communications that are short, simple, and attention-getting.

Owners and Employees of Businesses

Individual members of the community audience may well be one and the same as the business audience, but when they interact with schools or centers on behalf of their companies, they have different concerns. The primary benefit companies get from education programs is the same as the rest of society—the "product" of educated, contributing adults—but their perception of those benefits is more specific. Today's children are tomorrow's workforce. With this in mind, companies often support scholarships or promote programs to enhance student skills and interest in subject areas relevant to the firm's particular needs. For example, a chemical firm may sponsor a national science fair; an engineering firm may sponsor a math program for gifted middle school students. Will the winner of the middle school math competition end up working for this particular firm? Probably not—the firm is partially motivated by the idea that raising the level of math education overall will result in a better pool of potential employees and partially motivated simply by the high value it places on that skill area. It may also see the sponsorship as a chance to build a positive image with a group of students likely to become leaders in that industry. These benefits are long-range, intangible, and indirect, based more in core values than in any personal benefit. Just as with the parents who don't see the learning experience as a key benefit of the afterschool care program, this is a case where the audience may not be fully aware of the benefit or, at least, may need some prompting to remind them of the benefit.

A secondary benefit for this audience is that companies tend to wish to be perceived as helpful and cooperative members of their community. Because this benefit is more immediate and direct, it is more obvious and relevant to the audience.

For the business audience, another secondary benefit of interacting with schools and centers is personal satisfaction for the individual employees involved in that interaction. People have a natural tendency to want to encourage future members of their own profession and to share their own experiences with youngsters. They may feel good about volunteering to put on a math competition and seeing children's budding interest in higher-level mathematics or about giving a preschool group a tour of the lab and sparking interest in science.

When communicating with this audience, it is important to keep these benefits in mind and to focus the audience's attention on them as well. Educators and companies share the same beliefs in the primary benefit of an educated society, although the role of education in that picture is more salient for educators! But it is important for educators to recognize that positive presentation of the company as a corporate citizen and personal satisfaction for employees may be more salient and powerful benefits for companies and the individuals who represent them.

In addition to keeping communications short, simple, and attention-getting, communications for business audiences need to highlight those benefits specifically relevant to the firm or profession. Photographs of employees interacting with students, children's work with captions that connect to future careers, or thank-you notes produced by students to the company that can be shared publicly are all ways to focus on these benefits. As will be discussed in Strategy Two, "Invest in the Most Credible Communicators," it is also important to use cues and communication styles that business audiences will decode as professional and competent in direct communications—professional dress, business cards, and correspondence typed on letterhead.

Other Educators

It is easy to forget to be strategic when reaching out to other educators because we see them as part of us or on our side, but in fact strategy can be especially important when reaching out to other educators. For principals, the school boards, other principals in the district, and teachers they supervise are key audiences. For teachers, their principals, school boards, and other teachers are key audiences. Communicating with these audiences of other educators can be very important because they make decisions about curriculum, funding, support resources, and teaching methods. For afterschool and extracurricular learning programs, schools and teachers are a key audience. They may be a major source of referrals. Audiences of other educators are also important because they are educators themselves. Their attitudes about curriculum and teaching methods influence the way they work with children. Influencing educators' attitudes can have multiplying effects on children's learning.

All too often, communication pieces are not specifically designed for other educators. For example, a teacher creates a hallway display primarily intended for parents. Her colleagues and principal also see it, but the display does not address their concerns about the teaching method. Even when other educators are the primary intended audience, it is too easy to save time by reusing communication designed for other audiences, such as taking a parent-night documentation display to a conference. Because of their profession, other educators probably have some background information already, and they are particularly interested in pedagogical implications. A communication designed for parents likely spends too much time or space on background information and very little time or space on pedagogical implications. One problem with this is simply that the communication is not very effective for audiences of educators. In many cases, this is not so harmful since other educators were merely an incidental audience anyway.

When dealing with educator audiences as incidental audiences—meaning they will see communications intended for someone else—one solution is to provide additional information in a way that does not detract from the meaning of the message for the primary audience. For example, if a documentation display intended for parents is to be placed in the hallway, a separate note could be sent to teachers and the principal, calling attention to this display and making a few key points about pedagogical implications. A handout for educators could be made available near the display that would provide this information.

When dealing with educator audiences as a primary audience, it is a good idea to customize the communication piece if possible to call attention to your voice as a professional and the audience's role as professionals. Once your audience gets into professional mode, they are more motivated to make the effort to think in-depth and more open to looking for ideas for their own teaching. It also builds the relationship between the audience and communicator as colleagues. When your audience is aware of you as a fellow teacher, that audience is more likely to respond with the support and synergistic ideas of a real learning community. Developing this kind of professional relationship is probably a major reason for sharing the documentation in the first place.

When reaching out to fellow educators, consider that they will be much more interested in their col- leagues' professional growth and development than a lay audience would be. Personal stories of a teacher's growth, struggles to overcome challenges, and mo- ments of insight will likely be meaningful and inter- esting to audiences of educators. These stories are personally relevant for fellow educators because they share common experiences. Including these stories can keep the professional portion of communication aimed at fellow educators from becoming too dry or academic. It is a chance to share your passion. It is also a chance to add interest and engage your audience of colleagues.

FOR ANY AUDIENCE, the key to reaching them is to step into their shoes. Consider who they are, what they need to know, how they could benefit from the infor- mation presented, and how the communication piece would look to them.

CHAPTER 5

Strategy 2

Invest in the Most Credible Communicators: Teachers, Principals, and Children

Credibility—the quality or power of inspiring belief (Webster's Ninth New Collegiate Dictionary, 1990)

THE ISSUE OF CREDIBILITY has intrigued communication scholars and professional persuaders since Aristotle. The content of a message just doesn't matter very much if the audience does not believe the speaker (or writer or presenter). As Bert Decker noted in his popular book, *You've Got to Be Believed to Be Heard* (1991), before people are ready to think about a message, they need to know that the speaker is worth listening to.

Public relations strategy emphasizes the importance of letting the most credible communicators do the talking. Company "spokespeople," as public relations professionals are often labeled in news stories, are credible enough to report on basic facts about the company or to share prepared statements, but no one really believes they know the chemistry behind the product or understand what it's really like to work on the assembly line. For the real meat of the story, we expect to hear quotes from CEOs, expert engineers, or workers with firsthand experience. No amount of communication skill can replace credibility built on expertise and trustworthiness.

Teachers, principals, and children are worth listening to—they are the ones who can tell the real story about schools! Communication scholars and professionals have identified ways in which people decide who to believe, and those findings show teachers and principals have a significant credibility advantage when they are talking about what children are learning. Two types of credibility have been identified: initial (established before a communication) and terminal (established after the communication) (Hamilton & Parker, 1993). Both types depend on audience members' subjective perceptions—there is no "real" measure of credibility because each audience member has his or her own opinion.

HIGH INITIAL CREDIBILITY

If the communicator and listeners already know each other, initial credibility is based on that relationship. When the communicator and listeners do not know each other, initial credibility is often based on a few known facts about the communicator. Because of this, communicators are usually introduced by providing facts about their credibility. For example, expert speakers are often introduced by a separate speech outlining their credentials. News stories mention the job title or other qualification of the quoted speakers as part of the attribution: "City engineer John Jones said . . . ." "Mary Smith, who saw the accident, said . . . ." Sometimes these credibility factors are established unconsciously because of the situation. For example, movie theater customers will believe the show is sold out simply because the person who said so is wearing a movie theater uniform and is standing behind the cashier's window—who said it is often so convincing that no evidence is required. Teachers and principals have high initial credibility because of their jobs and the assumptions people associate with those jobs.

Communication scholars have identified two major components of credibility: expertise and trustworthiness (Petty & Cacioppo, 1981).

Expertise

Although teachers may not think of themselves as experts, they are experts in education in the most traditional sense of the term *expert*—especially in comparison with many of the people they may be communicating with, such as parents or members of the community. People expect that most teachers have a college degree in education and have studied how students learn and ways to measure what students are learning. People expect that teachers have continued learning about how to do their jobs better through seminars and reading. In addition to a degree, people will frequently assume that teachers have some kind of state certification, which means an independent third party has certified that they have achieved a certain standard level of knowledge and skills. When individuals are providing instruction in another setting, such an ice rink or botanical center, assumptions are made that they have expertise in that area or they would not have been selected to teach the class.

Yet expertise is broader than academic knowledge. Experts are people who know about a subject, and that knowledge can come from a variety of sources. In engaged learning methods such as the Project Approach, the "experts" young children consult may be waitresses, janitors, or 1st graders. Likewise, adults frequently turn to eyewitnesses or older, more experienced sources for credible information. Although people tend to associate the term *expertise* with academic knowledge, experience is often even more valuable to people than "book learning."

Firsthand experience is a powerful and convincing source of expertise. Who is better qualified to speak about the learning that is going on in classrooms than the teachers, who work directly with the children? Teachers personally observe the activities of children and are eyewitnesses to children's progress daily.

Academic expertise makes teachers' firsthand experience even more credible, because teachers know what to look for. Imagine that an eyewitness to a crime happens to be a detective or police officer: The court case would probably go smoothly because that particular eyewitness would likely have noticed more useful details than the average person might see. Likewise, teachers have the skill to perceive children's activities as evidence of the learning and emotional development that is occurring. Teachers are also focused on perceiving children as learners. Even though they may spend less time with their students than the students' parents, teachers may be able to report more direct observations of learning.

Yet perhaps there are people who witnessed that learning even more directly—the children themselves. While children may lack other types of expertise, they are uniquely qualified to say what is going on in their heads. Students do not typically make lists of the skills they've acquired and may not even be aware of their own progress. Yet their activities and work speak volumes about their accomplishments. Part of the power of documentation as evidence stems from the fact that it is as close as we can get to what is going on in children's heads. Furthermore, on occasion students *do* evaluate their own progress in their own words, and engaged learning methods often encourage this valuable learning experience. Whether from a 5th grader's journal entry or a preschooler's quotes recorded by a teacher, students' own reports of their learning are highly credible.

Remember that credibility is an audience member's subjective perception about a communicator. Some people value academic study highly. Others see life and work experience as the most meaningful type of expertise. Regardless of individual philosophies about this, almost everyone finds a combination of direct involvement, formal training, and substantial work experience to be highly convincing.

Trustworthiness

Communication scholars have identified the other major component of credibility as trustworthiness, sometimes referred to as character or ethos. Expertise tells the audience member *if* the speaker can tell the truth. Trustworthiness focuses on whether he or she *will* tell the truth. Trustworthiness is based on an audience's perception of the personal integrity and impartiality of the communicator. Subjective as trustworthiness is, the lack of it effectively prevents meaningful persuasive communication. As history has shown, even someone with as much expertise as the president of the United States can hardly convince anyone of anything once he is perceived to be unworthy of trust.

Unless the communicator and audience already know each other, the audience's perception of the communicator as trustworthy may be weak initially. It may be based on simple nonverbal cues such as eye contact, a gut feeling, or basic assumptions about humanity. As long as someone has little to gain from lying, people tend to presume he or she would tell the truth. Teachers and principals have some advantages in this regard. The general perception of the profession is as being fairly trustworthy (imagine the challenge facing lawyers, advertisers, or politicians), and many people presume teachers and principals chose their profession out of love for children.

BUILDING ON CREDIBILITY

As defined earlier, strategic communication is communication designed to achieve goals. One of those goals is to build credibility. This not only increases the likelihood of convincing the audience of the message, but it also improves terminal credibility. Terminal credibility refers to the audience members' perception of the communicator's credibility after reading the newsletter or field trip note, looking at the display, or listening to a conversation. This is especially important with repeat audiences, such as parents, because the terminal credibility established in the first communication becomes the initial credibility for the second. There's nothing really terminal about it!

Trustworthiness in particular can be strengthened through communication and relationships over time. To establish trustworthiness, communicators need to show they are fair, open-minded, and honest. They also need to show they genuinely care about the audience, respect the audience's perspective, and have the audience's best interests at heart.

In everyday conversation, people naturally make frequent efforts to build their credibility by emphasizing their expertise and trustworthiness. "I've been doing this for 10 years, and it always works for me." "You know I wouldn't exaggerate about something this important." "All the studies show children need . . ."

When taking the communication process off automatic and making it strategic, it is possible to deliberately incorporate those credibility-building factors into communications such as a newsletter article, display, or presentation to parents or the school board.

Be Professional

Demonstrating professionalism, or behaving in a manner that signals to the audience that as an educator you take your job seriously, builds both components of credibility. First, conveying a professional attitude subtly reminds your audience that you have had specific training and experience, which build the expertise component of credibility. Second, demonstrating professionalism subtly implies that you are committed to your job, that you see your job as a mission larger than yourself, and that you subscribe to a set of ethics generally shared among other members of your profession. All of these combine to build trustworthiness.

Major mistakes in professionalism, on the other hand, can be detrimental to audience perceptions about both expertise and trustworthiness. If audience members, such as parents, concerned citizens, or school board members, see a grammatical error on a documentation display, they may conclude (even if only subconsciously) that the teacher has poor writing skills. If the teacher can't write well, maybe his education wasn't so extensive. If he can't write, what other important things might he not know? Parents and concerned citizens often expect near-perfection from those charged with teaching and setting examples for their children, and seemingly trivial mistakes people make all the time can become major credibility issues.

Alternatively, the audience may see the grammatical error as evidence that the teacher or principal does not take the job seriously. If he doesn't care about doing this display correctly, what else does he not really care about? This undermines the trustworthiness aspect of credibility. Running a spell-check and grammar-check in word-processing programs and double-checking spelling on displays can avoid this. The larger the letters, the easier it is to misspell or repeat words and the more prominent the mistake will be. Strategy Six, "Follow Design Conventions," discusses design techniques for making school communications look professional, and Chapter 12, Tools for Opening Windows, provides tips for making professional design quick and automatic.

Professionalism becomes a special issue when dealing with upper-level businesspeople. The profession of teaching involves looking approachable to children and parents—not to mention at times sitting on the floor, pasting, painting, playing with play-dough, and serving recess duty. The teaching and business professions rely on different signals to convey a sense of professionalism. When teachers or principals are dealing with members of the business community, they can build credibility by making an extra effort to convey signals the business community recognizes. Some parents and community members may also be business professionals and may respond well to a professional approach.

Dressing professionally (no child-oriented jumpers) and offering a business card at adult events are two easy ways to build credibility. Business cards serve a very practical purpose: They provide all the information needed to contact an educator and get the name and title correct in a convenient form that many businesspeople file directly into their address books. Teachers might want to include their home phone number and/or hours they can receive calls at school if this is permitted. Providing an e-mail address may make it convenient for project partners in the business world to reach teachers during business hours. Business cards are also very useful to provide to journalists and members of the media. Most office supply stores sell sheets of business cards to print on a laser printer and punch out. This is an inexpensive way that a small program or even a teacher alone can produce small quantities of business cards. See the lists in Figures 5.1 and 5.2 for further aides to looking professional.

Mention Credentials

One way to build credibility is to draw the audience's attention to your expertise. For a teacher or principal, this can be as simple as putting graduate degree initials or certification information on business cards or in a signature. Again, different audiences attach different values to academic credentials and experience. This technique works best for audiences who respect academic credentials but do not find them intimidating, such as school board members,

business managers, and some parents. For other parents, especially those who do not have much education themselves, a better method might be to include a little background about your teaching experience in your first newsletter or mention your background when introducing yourself to parents for the first time.

Credit Research Sources

Another way to build credibility is to borrow credibility from others by mentioning the articles or

Figure 5.1. Checklist for looking professional.

Does your program look professional?

- ✓ Business cards
- ✓ Letterhead
- ✓ Handouts or brochures summarize teaching philosophy
- ✓ Website is current, functional, and emphasizes student learning
- ✓ Program materials and displays emphasize learning
- ✓ Graphics add meaning—use a logo or children's work instead of clip art

Figure 5.2. Looking professional on a budget.

Looking professional on a budget

- Use a black-and-white letterhead that can be produced on a laser printer or copier
- Instead of color or professional printing, make formal letters, brochures, and handouts look distinctive by consistently using a distinctive paper—neutral tones or subtle visual texture such as granite, speckles, marble, or parchment. Office supply stores have lots in stock; coordinating papers (card stock, note cards, business cards, envelopes) can often be ordered online.
- Teachers can easily design their own business card and print small quantities as needed using Microsoft Publisher templates and punch-out business cards sheets available at any office supply store. Or a program can provide a business card template and the punch-card sheets to staff for a consistent look.
- Create an electronic version of the letterhead in a template or graphic and make it widely available to staff. The letterhead can be printed along with their documents. Not only is this cheaper, but it is also easier—no fussing with changing the printer paper or getting it pointed in the right direction.
- Create an electronic version of the logo or other graphics and make it widely available to staff so it can be easily added to documents and displays.
- Create letterhead note cards to use for notes home or thank-you notes. Standard-size sheets with punch-out postcards are available at any office store and can be used either for printing postcards on a computer or for printing a supply of blank letterhead note cards to keep on hand for handwritten notes.

books that information came from. For example, in a newsletter article explaining the service learning approach to parents, a leading book on the subject can be quoted or paraphrased and cited. This builds both components of credibility in several ways. First, the information becomes more credible because it comes from someone with a higher level of expertise than you may have. Second, the audience's perception of your expertise improves because you've demonstrated you did research on the topic. Third, the audience's perception of your trustworthiness goes up because (1) you cared enough to research, (2) you are confident enough about your information to let them check your sources, and (3) you respect their expertise enough to think they might be interested in your sources. Again, for some audiences such as school board members, an academic quote and citation might be most meaningful. For other audiences, such as parents, it might be more effective to have a "How Can I Find Out More?" section in a classroom newsletter. While it is certainly true that few people would seek out the book or article, it helps credibility to make the information available.

Teachers, principals, and other school staff who have brochures or handouts on hand explaining the engaged learning approaches used in a school or classroom should definitely try to refer to some outside research supporting the approach and suggest some places to go for additional information. For schoolwide programs, it can also be helpful to borrow from the credibility of local leaders such as principals, school board leaders, city officers, or prominent businesspeople by including quotes supporting the teaching approach.

Show You Care

Showing your excitement about children's learning not only engages those listening or reading but also builds trustworthiness. Comments such as "We are all so excited about our trip to learn about the bank" or "I was so proud to see how much Jose's writing had improved" can be easily added to a school board or parent night presentation or a field trip letter. Letting genuine and natural enthusiasm show does not detract from professionalism. Sharing your enthusiasm lets your audiences feel a bit more like they know you as a person as well as demonstrating you care about your subject.

Speak Like You Mean It

During a presentation, making eye contact and speaking with conviction enhance credibility. Even though people try to be understanding about nervousness, they still unconsciously make credibility judgments based on nonverbal cues such as a speaker's eye contact and fidgeting. It is much more important to appear engaged and confident than to use any particular phrasing or to cover absolutely everything you had planned, so use minimal notes to keep yourself from reading. Focus on making your audience understand what is happening with the children. Don't let your nerves weaken your credibility!

Strategy Seven, "Reach Out to the Media," provides additional public relations techniques to prepare teachers, principals, and students to share learning experiences more effectively. One technique that is commonly used by professional communicators to keep speaking focused and flexible is a list of talking points. Guidelines for developing talking points are included in Chapter 11, Foundation Builders.

Respect Your Audience

Studies have shown that trustworthiness becomes even more important when the audience is personally involved with the subject (Petty & Cacioppo, 1981). No one is more deeply personally involved than a parent with his or her child, so trustworthiness may be more important than expertise for parents.

People tend to trust people they like, and people tend to like people who understand them and like them back. Showing respect for your audience and understanding of their needs and concerns (discussed in Strategy One, "Analyze Your Audience") is essential for building trust. While it is important to demonstrate expertise, it is far more important to demonstrate respect. Never make your audience feel stupid. Always speak or write at a level that your audience can understand. Educational jargon should be avoided with any audience that might not be familiar with those vocabulary terms. At the same time, don't underestimate or "talk down" to your audience. The solution is to find plain-language ways to express the full ideas behind what you want to communicate about children's learning. It is better to convey one or two ideas well than to rely on jargon to conserve space. Respect your audience by showing that you believe that you and they have a common concern for children's learning and that you believe they can understand what you are trying to communicate about how children learn.

INVEST IN CREDIBILITY

Strategy Two is to invest in the most credible communicators to tell how students are learning: teachers, principals, and the children themselves (see Figure 5.3). Educators can invest in those communicators in three ways:

1. Let them speak (or write, share work, or be quoted)—to take advantage of educators' high initial credibility.
2. Build credibility strategically by deliberately mentioning factors that help audiences recognize their expertise and trustworthiness. Teachers, principals, and students are the best-qualified communicators to help people understand what is really going on in our schools because they are the most believable.
3. Provide training and support so they will feel comfortable in sharing their expertise.

Figure 5.3. Why educators make credible communicators.

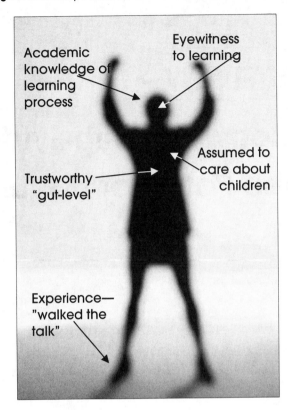

CHAPTER 6

Strategy 3

Convince with Evidence: The Power of Documentation

Evidence—1. an outward sign; 2. proof, testimony

Proof—1. the evidence that compels acceptance by the mind of a truth or fact (*Webster's Ninth New Collegiate Dictionary*, 1990)

EVIDENCE OR PROOF is a key component of persuasive communication. Individuals' decisions to be convinced or influenced by a message depend on many factors, but their evaluation of evidence is a primary factor. We demand evidence before we are convinced. Our society accepts many types of evidence—examples; stories; quotations; expert opinions; typical or ordinary opinions; photographs and illustrations; and formal research studies such as experiments, statistics, polls, sound recordings, demonstrations, firsthand experience, and so forth. Standardized tests are one form of evidence of children's learning that have become widely accepted by the general public, but they are not the only form of evidence that is gathered and shared—grades, awards, performances, competitions, and documentation are other forms of evidence. This chapter will show that documentation is a particularly powerful type of evidence that can be highly convincing, memorable, and even inspiring.

Perhaps the most common example of the use of evidence to convince is the criminal jury trial. In the trial process we can see two distinct uses of evidence. First, detectives gather evidence in order to determine the truth. They systematically collect outward signs (fingerprints, witness testimony, receipts) and then evaluate and interpret those signs to come to their own conclusions. Next, the prosecutor reviews that same evidence to select the most convincing items to present to the jury. With the goal of obtaining a guilty verdict, the prosecutor strategically constructs an argument or case, using the most convincing pieces of evidence to prove each claim. The prosecutor emphasizes evidence the jurors will be able to remember and repeat during jury deliberations, evidence that will not only convince individual jurors but that those jurors can use to convince their fellow jurors.

What makes some evidence more effective than other evidence? Professional communicators spend a great deal of time and energy selecting just the right piece of evidence for each situation. Different types of evidence have their own strengths and weaknesses. The most effective evidence will be convincing (logically perceived as proof), powerful (engaging, memorable, and even inspiring), and convenient (easy to obtain, interpret, and explain).

Western society holds formal studies, such as experiments and statistics, in high esteem, and standardized test scores fit this category of evidence. Quantified measures—*statistics*—have several strengths. A major strength of statistics as a form of evidence is that they summarize large quantities of information to permit efficient analysis of broad patterns—this is why we love them! Instead of looking at 100 individual questions, we look at a total score; instead of looking at 100 individual students, we look at an average; instead of looking at individual cases, we look at patterns and trends.

Statistics are a powerful analytical tool, and, as a form of evidence, they have characteristics that make them convincing and convenient as well. Statistics are convincing because they are widely perceived as objective and unbiased. Educators familiar with the challenge of designing an effective, unbiased test and interpreting test results know the picture is far more complex, but the fact remains that standardized tests are widely *perceived* as highly credible, even indisputable, evidence.

Journalists are accustomed to using statistics, such as the U.S. Census, the FBI crime report for their towns, leading local employers' annual corporate reports, or a local "school report card" that gives the public a regular status report. Newly released results of a study are considered newsworthy, and the reports serve as a convenient reference throughout the year. This use of statistics is not just for media. Corporations distribute their quarterly reports of earnings to stockholders; schools distribute their annual test results to parents and legislators. Because of these strengths, professional communicators—journalists, public relations practitioners, advertisers, political speechwriters, lobbyists—frequently use statistical evidence.

Statistical evidence of children's learning has many strengths, but it also has limitations. Educators know standardized tests have limited power as a teaching and evaluation tool, but, as professional communicators know, the power of statistics also has limitations as a form of evidence. Standardized test scores emphasize comparisons with norms that may or may not be relevant to the characteristics of the local community. The reporting of results of standardized test scores usually focuses more on performance at the time the test was taken. This performance may be lower, or higher, than norms. Less attention is paid to growth or progress of individual students or even a school over time—certainly individual progress is not emphasized. This can be misleading, especially when a school or program has high mobility rates among the student body.

Statistics are convenient and convincing, but their power is limited. They are not very engaging or memorable, and they are certainly not very inspiring. When using statistics in newspapers and other media, professional communicators turn to other forms of evidence—photographs, stories, inspiring quotations—to bring issues to life. While these types of evidence do not efficiently capture broad patterns as statistics do, they provide details the statistics do not. Professional communicators have found that these other forms of evidence are more meaningful to varied audiences and more likely to capture their attention. In educational programs, documentation has the potential to be a powerful source of evidence because it can be engaging, memorable, and inspiring as well as logically convincing.

DOCUMENTATION IS CONVINCING

The beauty of statistics is that they reduce information to a brief, efficient summary. However, the helpfulness of summaries is limited. Documentation provides a comprehensive, in-depth picture of the learning progress of an individual child or a group of children. The beauty of documentation and qualitative sources of evidence is that they provide a significant quantity and variety of information that then offers extensive opportunities for analysis of multiple facets of development and learning. Teachers, parents, and researchers can review the same collection or piece of documentation many times and still find new insight. Academics call this "rich data."

Documentation Captures Thinking

Documentation provides insight into students' thought processes. An understanding of how a child came to a particular conclusion can show significant learning progress and creative problem solving even when the "answer" is officially wrong. Documentation also gives the audience an appreciation for how children think and how children's thinking is different from that of adults. They can experience the challenge and wonder along with the child. For example, during a project about farms at Discovery Preschool, children made a model farm. As often occurs in project work by young children, the construction of a model poses many opportunities for problem solving and development of skills. The teacher documented a problem encountered when a child used clothespins to represent cornstalks and then discovered that they would not stand up when they were placed where the cornfield should go in the model farm. Through persistence and problem solving with a friend, this child was able to solve the problem independently without an adult (see Color Plate 1). These thought processes—assessing a problem, designing a solution, trying it out, and persisting to find a better solution—are, in fact, a major part of many disciplines of study.

Schools endeavor not only to convey facts but also to facilitate the development of habits of thinking for lifelong learning, such as creative problem solving, critical thinking, and being persistent. School goals and standards primarily emphasize the development of skills and knowledge. Yet tests focusing solely on answers and outcomes indicate these thinking habits only by measuring the results of thinking. Documentation can actually directly capture these thinking processes.

Quotations from children are one powerful way of indicating what they are thinking. Another effective way thought processes are captured is telling the story of children's efforts to answer a particular question or solve a particular problem. For example, Color Plate 2 tells the story of toddlers solving a problem during a project. This story was told on a panel for parents and teachers to show how children as young as age 2 could work together and participate in project work. The center faced a critical communication challenge when it wanted to convert a Mom's Day Out program, which was perceived as a babysitting service, to an educational program for toddlers. This panel helped current and prospective parents understand that experiences occurring in a program for toddlers at Northminster Learning Center are educational.

Documentation that captures children's thinking:

- *Includes evidence of thoughts*, not just samples of children's work

Documentation Provides Many Views

Professional communicators know that multiple sources and types of evidence are more convincing than a single source. One reason is that audiences cannot easily discount evidence as an artifact of a particular method or bias when a whole collection of indicators or viewpoints supports the same claims. Another is that different audience members may find different evidence to be especially convincing. One person may rely on expert credentials; another may respond better to visual information. Thus, integrating multiple types of evidence can reach more audience members. Documentation includes multiple sources and types of evidence such as photographs, recordings or quotations of children's conversation, journal entries, samples of writing, drawings, sculptures, and models. For example, when Northminster Learning Center wanted to communicate to parents that afterschool programs are learning experiences, director Stacy Berg created several documentation panels on the children's study of insects. Figure 6.1 shows the first of these panels.

Documentation that uses multiple sources:

- *Shares a variety of types of documentation* in displays, newsletters, or presentations
- *Subtly signals the audience* that the examples shared are just a few pieces of a large collection of evidence

The Evidence Speaks for Itself

Nothing is more convincing than the conclusions we draw ourselves, based on our own evaluations of the evidence. Documentation often allows viewers to have the sense that they are evaluating children's work for themselves—children's progress is often so evident that even someone not used to looking at student work can easily recognize it. Time 1 and time 2 drawings are a very powerful piece of evidence. The progress illustrated is not merely recognizable but often amazing. The two paintings in Figure 6.2 show remarkable progress in the child's understanding of a bee. The panel presenting these two paintings indicates that these were painted only hours apart by the same child. The first was painted when she studied bees by looking at pictures in books. The second was painted after the children observed bees in the field and the teacher captured one of the bees in a jar so they could study it closely. The panel challenges the viewer to draw conclusions from this evidence about how children learn best.

Documentation that lets the audience draw conclusions:

- Has documentation where *progress is striking and easily recognized*
- *Has documentation that seems direct and unmediated*—the child's own drawing, direct quotes from children—rather than relying on teacher description

Documentation Is Scientific

Often documentation is part of portfolios, which are systematically collected on a regular basis, offering a rich, comprehensive picture of an individual child's progress and of the progress of a class as a whole. When teachers evaluate progress based on documentation, they draw on scientifically established national norms—norms of child development established through academic scholarship and, in some cases, by formal documentation systems such as Work Sampling. Teachers also draw on their own sense of norms developed through years of teaching experience.

While statistics are widely accepted in our society as "scientific"—objective, systematic, and sophisticated—a layperson may not recognize those characteristics in documentation at first glance. Even as educators use documentation as evidence of children's learning, they may also want to communicate that documentation itself is a scientific approach. One way documentation is shown as systematic is to document the system itself—if the school uses forms as a shortcut for filing documentation, the school may exhibit some documentation complete with the form and teacher notes. Part of a standards checklist is enlarged on a copier with the relevant items checked as part of the documentation display previously presented in Color Plate 1. Another way to show that documentation is systematic is to provide optional information about the documentation system, such as a stack of brochures next to a documentation display or included with a press release, or a web link to background information on the documentation system the school uses.

Documentation that appears scientifically based:

- *Refers to norms and benchmarks* to help the audience place the documentation in context
- Lets the audience know that *documentation is a systematic process*

DOCUMENTATION IS POWERFUL

Evidence is powerful when it is engaging, memorable, and inspiring. While statistics are convincing and convenient, they are not powerful. Professional communicators seek other forms of evidence to really get their messages across.

Documentation Is Engaging

No one can be persuaded without paying attention, and our attention is drawn to what is interesting. Documentation is inherently interesting. People are drawn to vivid photos, drawings, odd-looking three-dimensional sculptures, and things that can be experienced through all five senses—things that can be touched, heard, smelled or tasted as well as merely read. Stories, questions, and glimpses of character are what most capture human interest. Documentation includes engaging evidence.

Documentation that is engaging:

- *Emphasizes photos, drawings, and other visually interesting forms of children's work.* By making them

large relative to blocks of text, these illustrations draw the eye even before people have decided to read the newsletter or give the display a closer look.
- *Has close-up photos of people.* From our earliest experiences as infants, we are drawn to human faces and expressions. A child's fascination and curiosity are often captivatingly visible in a close-up photo but lost in the clutter of a large-group photo.
- *Tells stories.* A favorite of professional communicators, stories have characters, plot (involving some kind of conflict or question), and resolution. Even a very short, simple story can be powerful (think of the 30-second television commercial). Stories can focus on an individual child's growth or a group's struggle to make their sculpture stand up, or they can invite the audience to join the children in solving the mystery of where the school buses go during the daytime. Documentation can also include stories that students have dictated or written.
- *Asks questions.* When viewing displays, such as in museums, people read questions aloud, sometimes even when they are alone, and will try to find the answers to the questions.
- *Uses real objects* with dimension and texture rather than drawings or photos when possible.
- *If possible and relevant, has opportunities for the audience to taste or smell things.* When taste, smell, or touch is an important part of the children's learning experience but it's not convenient for audiences to actually taste or touch, other ways to share the children's experience—such as a photo of children holding their noses–invite the audience to imagine the sensation.

Documentation Is Memorable

Evidence that is engaging, as described above, also tends to be memorable. In particular, anything a communicator can do to increase the audience's thinking about the message improves memory. The more time people spend generating their own thoughts about something, the more likely they are to remember it. Because people spend more time thinking about things that attract their attention, they are more likely to remember them as well.

There is more thought involved (and more commitment to the resulting attitude) when people have drawn conclusions for themselves rather than simply reading an answer. This means information presented

Figure 6.1. Panel on afterschool learning. Director Stacy Berg created this display on an insect project by the afterschool program to help parents understand the value of high-quality educational experiences after school.

Are Children Interested in

As children began to arrive from school, they were fascinated by a katydid. They observed it for a long period of time and completed some initial sketches. This led to a study of many different insects.

Project Summary

Class: After School Program

Age: Kindergarten-Fifth After School
Students

Teachers: Stacy Berg, Jaime Swick,
Michelle Herington, Judy Hultgren

Length of the Project: 6 weeks

Size of Class: 30 students

Children's List of Questions:

- *Do ants really have stingers?*
- *Why do bees buzz?*
- *How do spiders make their webs?*
- *How do butterflies get different colors?*
- *Why are some bugs poisonous?*
- *How come spiders don't have wings?*
- *How many kinds of butterflies are in the world?*
- *What does a butterfly eat?*
- *How come spiders are called arachnids?*
- *Why do mealworms have 13 segments?*
- *Are there more than two colors of walking sticks?*
- *How come monarch butterflies have so many spots?*
- *How do bees make honey?*
- *How do bees make hives?*
- *How do bees go to the bathroom?*

The Dragonfly

This event was an example of children developing intrapersonal and interpersonal skills. The multi-age learning group learned a lesson in cooperation and learning groups in this series. The group first showed the learning disposition of persistence as they spent a great deal of time trying to catch the dragonfly as a group.

After catching the dragonfly, I observed the group struggle to work together but as they failed the dragonfly flew away. After initial frustration I encouraged the group to think about how they could work together and contribute a skill to ensure a successful capture.

On the second attempt to catch and transfer the dragonfly, the children huddled together and made a plan for each child (ex. holding the net, holding the box, etc.) to help get the dragonfly in the box. Through the cooperation of 1st, 2nd, 3rd, and special need students, the group was successful in adding the dragonfly to their insect collection.

The group makes an attempt to catch a dragonfly.

Each child trying to help in their own way allows the dragonfly to fly free.

After re-grouping, the team scoots together, assigns tasks, and captures the dragonfly.

Figure 6.1. (cont'd)

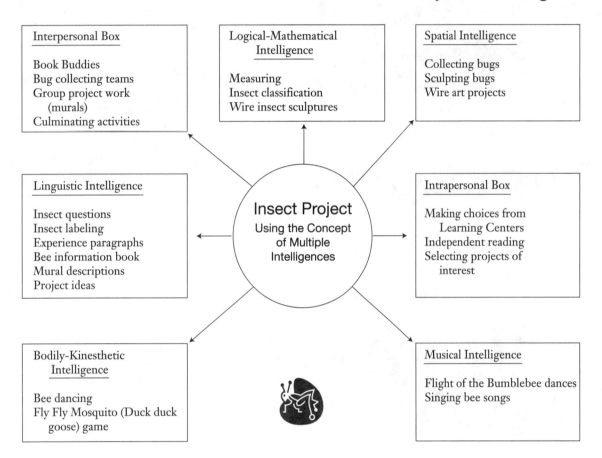

Learning <u>After</u> School?

The Insect Project had begun!

Interpersonal Box

Book Buddies
Bug collecting teams
Group project work
    (murals)
Culminating activities

**Logical-Mathematical
Intelligence**

Measuring
Insect classification
Wire insect sculptures

Spatial Intelligence

Collecting bugs
Sculpting bugs
Wire art projects

Linguistic Intelligence

Insect questions
Insect labeling
Experience paragraphs
Bee information book
Mural descriptions
Project ideas

Insect Project
Using the Concept
of Multiple
Intelligences

Intrapersonal Box

Making choices from
    Learning Centers
Independent reading
Selecting projects of
    interest

**Bodily-Kinesthetic
Intelligence**

Bee dancing
Fly Fly Mosquito (Duck duck
    goose) game

Musical Intelligence

Flight of the Bumblebee dances
Singing bee songs

The first of many drawings and
writing opportunities that
occurred in this project

Figure 6.2. Bee painting one and two. Four-year-old Maddie painted the first bee from knowledge gained from books and discussion in the classroom. Maddie painted the second bee just a few hours later after seeing a bee fly and capturing it to study. This documentation shows the value of concrete, hands-on experiences for children.

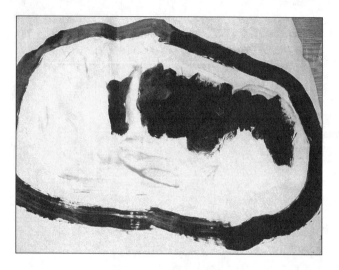

Documentation Is Inspiring

Through documentation, outsiders can share in the actual learning experience of students—their excitement, their frustrations, and their triumphs. These glimpses of child experiences can be heartwarming. Documentation can open a window to help people see the world through children's eyes and see children's learning through a teacher's eyes. Children's drawings, quotes, stories, and photos can communicate at an emotional level that statistics and grades can never attain. This emotional involvement is what gives people the energy to take action. That action could be as simple as an individual decision to spend extra time thinking about an issue and becoming strongly committed to an attitude, or as extensive as long-term organizational behavior changes. For example, a father might be inspired to spend an extra half-hour reading background information about the inquiry-based science teaching method used in his child's classroom, and over a day or two his thinking could lead him to become very supportive of the approach. This may have no immediate visible consequences beyond contributing to a positive parent–teacher partnership, but in the long term this father may find himself explaining the learning method to another parent or speaking up about its effectiveness as the school ponders whether to expand the use of the approach. He may also begin to use similar methods with his child at home. Or a businesswoman might be inspired by a documentation display to arrange for her company to develop a partnership to support science study at a local school.

All of the above positive characteristics of documentation depend on good choices of documentation to share. *Documentation that is engaging and memorable evidence* is also documentation that is inspiring.

HOW DOCUMENTATION IS USED

Using especially powerful documentation effectively depends also on how it is presented. The communicator must help the audience make the connection between the message and their own personal involvement. If inspiring further involvement is a key goal of the communication, it should not be left to chance. To maximize documentation's ability to inspire action, documentation should provide a way for that urge to translate into action.

Documentation which inspires action:

by raising a question or letting obvious conclusions go unstated (so the audience draws the conclusion) is often better remembered than information that is simply told to the audience. Any of the previously described characteristics of engaging documentation also help make the message more memorable.

Particularly memorable documentation:

- *Presents stories* in a conflict-resolution format
- *Presents information* by raising a question or letting obvious conclusions go unstated

- *Offers optional layers of information.* Much of the "action" is simply in form of increased thought and commitment to attitudes. This is facilitated by making additional information easily available to anyone who seeks it. When presented effectively, documentation offers optional layers of information. For example, a display can be accompanied by a brochure with background information about documentation or a school's engaged learning method; website displays can have a link for additional information. The background information can include a list of "further reading." A display of a classroom project can be accompanied by the class journal of the project and a few of the key books the children used. (This extra information should be optional so that the audience is not overwhelmed.)

- *Suggests ways people can help.* A parent newsletter can mention volunteer opportunities, supplies needed for the classroom, or ways parents can support the classroom experience with activities at home. A community display can suggest business partner opportunities or "volunteer grandparent" programs. If a documentation display is reaching different audiences, one corner of it might include a list of "What You Can Do" that could be changed for different audiences—emphasizing the business partner program when the display will be at the Chamber of Commerce meeting or the volunteer grandparent program when the display will be at the senior center. Gains from having more community members feeling supportive of and committed to a school may far exceed the actual hours of volunteer labor. Even *considering* making a donation or volunteering can make people feel they have a personal stake in the issue.

IS DOCUMENTATION CONVENIENT?

As pointed out earlier, three characteristics of good evidence are that it is convincing, powerful, and convenient. Documentation is clearly both convincing and powerful, but is it convenient as well? Is it easy to obtain, interpret, and understand?

Careful documentation of children's work can be time-consuming and expensive (photocopies, photo printing, and so forth). But the primary purpose of documenting student work is for teachers to monitor progress and guide the learning experience. Think back to the two purposes of evidence in a criminal case. First, the detectives gather evidence systematically in order to determine what happened: Was there a crime? Who are the suspects? After they have figured out what happened, the prosecutor selects a few choice bits from this large body of evidence to prove a case to the audience of jurors.

That first purpose, figuring out what happened, is the main reason teachers document children's work. What have the children learned? How can I help them reach their individual potential? How can I help the class reach the next level? Many teachers are already collecting a great deal of documentation for educational purposes. In that case, obtaining the documentation for strategic communication is easy for teachers, because it is being produced anyway.

This book does not advocate creating products expressly for the purpose of using them as a strategic communication tool. Documentation of student learning should already be occurring in good classrooms as a part of good teaching. Using it as evidence in strategic communication simply gets more value out of the time, energy, and expense already being invested in the learning process. In community programs providing educational services, such as art guilds or museums, documenting and collecting may not be part of their processes. In those cases, it will require extra effort. We can only assure you that the benefits of documentation will extend well beyond the purposes of strategic communication to program enhancement.

It does take extra time to carefully select documentation from a large collection to serve as convincing and powerful evidence in strategic communications, but the investment in time and production expenses is minimal compared with the potential gain in positive attitudes toward the school or institution and understanding of children's learning. This book contains numerous suggestions for time-saving shortcuts to minimize the time investment and production expenses while maximizing the impact on the audience.

Documentation is not as easy for those outside educational institutions to obtain. Reporters, legislators, school boards, private school advisory boards, and supporting institutions are accustomed to getting a regular report of standardized test scores. Established distribution systems are typically not in place for documentation. This does not mean that outside audiences are less interested in documentation, but it does mean that those on the front lines of student contact may need to make an extra effort to bring documentation and other evidence of children's learning to their attention.

INTERPRETING DOCUMENTATION

Documentation has the potential to be easy for the audience to interpret and understand, but this can also create a challenge for the strategic communicator. Our society is very accustomed to interpreting statistics such as standardized test scores—large quantities of information can be efficiently conveyed in a chart or in an average. It is not necessary to explain what an average is or outline the concept of testing; this background knowledge is assumed. This is not the case for documentation. Parents, community residents who don't have children of their own, and even teachers working with another grade level may need help to understand the learning represented by a particular piece of work. For example, the web page of the University Primary School's Project "Who Measures What in Our Neighborhood" (Hertzog & Klein, 2002) shows not only a sample of a student's time 1 and time 2 drawings, but also explains the purpose of the activity (see Figure 6.3). The explanation includes what the students did, what they learned, and the purpose for repeating the activity. Viewers were also able to see the result. When documentation is carefully selected and placed in context, it can be intuitively understood.

Documentation that bridges the gap:

- *Uses captions and titles to interpret* the learning represented by the documentation, not simply to label it.
- *Provides benchmarks and context.* For example, the caption for a kindergartner's drawing of a restaurant menu could point out that the menu shows inventive spelling, which is typical for the age and demonstrates how this is evidence of understanding how letters represent sounds. References add credibility.
- *Links the skills demonstrated by the documentation with the school's learning standards.* One convenient, highly effective way this is done on a stand-up display is to enlarge part of the school's standards checklist on a copier and check off the relevant items. Not only does this help the audience interpret the child's work, but it also sends the message that this is all part of a scientific system.
- *Provides the age of the child who did the work and sometimes the dates.* When showing progress over time, include the dates. People who are not used to working with young children are often amazed at how much progress can be made in a short time and how much children are capable of doing.

Figure 6.3. The teacher helps viewers understand the importance of observational drawing on this webpage from the University Primary School's "Who Measures What in Our Neighborhood" Project.

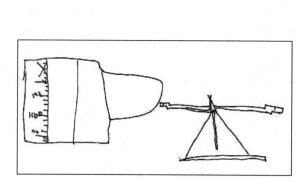

Time 1 Drawing--3/15/02
CS looks at measuring tools and makes an observational drawing of a timer and a balance scale.

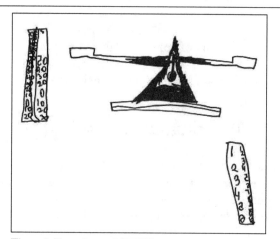

Time 2 Drawing--3/27/02
CS makes a more detailed drawing of the balance scale.

As students measured, they observed closely and investigated how the measurement tools worked. They made time 1 and time 2 observational drawings of items of interest. The purpose of doing a second observational drawing was to increase their ability to observe carefully and integrate more details into the drawings.

- *Presents examples of work before and after the learning experiences,* such as time 1 and time 2 drawings, knowledge webs constructed at the beginning and end of a project, or, for older children, research questions and outlines.

At first glance, documentation may not seem to be a very convenient form of evidence, but these challenges can be easily overcome to take full advantage of documentation's potential as a powerful and convincing source of evidence. Documentation is a convincing form of evidence of children's learning because it is strong enough evidence to speak for itself, it captures thought processes (not just outcomes), it measures learning using multiple methods and sources, and it is scientific. Documentation is powerful—engaging, memorable, and inspiring—because it opens a window on learning experiences, captivating audiences with human interest and imagination.

CHAPTER 7

Strategy 4

Plan Your Message: Deciding What to Say

DECIDING WHAT TO SAY may be the most challenging part of strategic communication. There is so much to say, especially if you have a lot of documentation worth sharing! But it is much better to deliver a few key messages well and actually transmit those messages than to take on too much and wind up not really communicating anything.

First, if a communicator tries to make too many main points and the communication or channel does not have enough space or time to provide convincing evidence for each point, the audience will not be persuaded. There is little to be gained from raising issues at all unless convincing evidence can be provided as well.

Second, if the audience does not remember those points, nothing has been gained. If there are too many points, an audience simply cannot remember them. For a short communication such as an open house display, the best a communicator can hope for is that the audience will remember a few main points—if those points are meaningful to the audience and if they are communicated in an effective and memorable way.

TWO KEYS TO PROFESSIONAL COMMUNICATIONS

Two keys to effective communication used by professional communicators are to choose the right message, one that is relevant for your audience, and to keep a tight focus on that one bite-sized message. This chapter starts by addressing these two keys for effective

communication and some tactics for keeping that tight focus. Later in the chapter, we discuss setting communication goals, including more in-depth discussion of choosing the right message.

Let's start with a close look at an example of effective strategic communication when Head Start teacher Rebecca Wilson of West Liberty Community Schools in Iowa shared her preschool children's house-building project at a parent night. The main channel of communication, and the climax of the parent-night event, was Ms. Wilson's PowerPoint presentation on the project. The houses the children built were also displayed that evening, along with some labels to help parents make sense of them. Ms. Wilson's PowerPoint slides appear in Figure 7.1. Keep in mind that this is the visual aid for a presentation only. It was not designed to stand alone but rather to be accompanied by Ms. Wilson's explanation, so we are reading it out of context. The first section of the presentation explained the Project Approach teaching method to parents. The second section showed how math and literacy goals were met through the project. Each section contained several clearly identified supporting points. The explanation of the Project Approach teaching method discusses five ways children learn through the project and provides several examples of each. For math and literacy goals, two or three skills are mentioned, with documentation examples that bring each to life.

The parent-night presentation provides an unusually pleasant communication situation for Ms. Wilson, relative to the situations many educators face. The

Figure 7.1. PowerPoint for parents of the house project. Teacher Rebecca Wilson designed this PowerPoint presentation about the House Project for parents to introduce the project approach as a teaching method. The presentation emphasizes development of math and literacy skills which she knows is important to the parents.

The House Project in a Dual Language Pre-Kindergarten Class

Roof

"Me in the house" -Blaine

Downstairs

Teacher: Rebecca Wilson
West Liberty Community Schools

1

What does my child do in a project?

- Formulates questions / *Hace preguntas*
- Draws / *Dibuja*
- Observes demonstrations / *Observa las demostraciones*
- Investigates / *Investiga*
- Represents learning / *Representa lo que aprendió*

2

Questions / Preguntas

Audrey: How do you make the walls? *¿Comó hacen las paredes?*
Simon, Oscar: How do you do the roof? *¿Comó hacen el techo?*
Ross: How do you do the floors? *¿Comó hacen el piso?*
Misael: What are the boards like? *¿Comó son las tablas?*
Ashton, Erica: How do you make the door? *¿Comó hacen las puertas?*
Christopher: Where do you buy wood at? *¿Dónde compran madera?*
Arianna: How do you fix the roof? *¿Como arreglan el techo?*
Juan Antonio: Do you use tape? *¿Usan cinta?*
Concepción: What are the boards for? *¿Para que son las tablas?*
Joshua, Juan Pablo: How do you build windows? *¿Comó construyen las ventanas?*

3

Drawing / Dibujar

- Fine motor skills
- Observational drawing / Dibujar de observación
- Memory drawing / *Dibujar de memoria*

Kyleigh drew the hammer – October 15th
Kyleigh dibujó el martillo – 15 de octubre

4

Oriana drew the safety goggles
Oriana dibujó los lentes

Concepción drew the screws
Concepción dibujó los tornillos

5

Memory Drawing

They loved the stairs!
¡Les gustaron las escaleras mucho!

Ashley's stairs

Felipe's door and stairs

6

Demonstrations / Demostrar

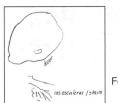

7

Demonstrations / Demostrar

"Quebra la tabla." Jose   "The roof top!" Kyleigh

8

Figure 7.1. (cont'd)

Mr. Koenig demonstrates to the AM class how walls are made.

Sr. Koenig enseña a la clase de la mañana como hacen las paredes de casas.

9

Investigation / Investigar

10

The children pass around the sanding block.
Los niños examinan el bloque con papel de lija.

11

- The afternoon class watches as workers re-roof a house near the school.
- *La clase de la tarde mira a unos trabajadores arreglando el techo de una casa cerca de la escuela.*

12

- The afternoon class examines different colors for kitchens at Zimmerman Homes.
- *En Zimmerman Homes la clase de la tarde examina los colores diferentes para las cocinas.* 13

Representation / Representar

Audrey suggested building the roof. When I asked her what she wanted to put on it, she said, "Shingles!"

Audrey me dijo que iba a poner "tablillas."

14

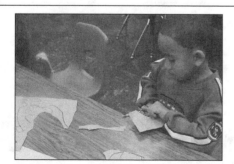

Oscar told me he wanted to put stairs in the house.
Oscar me dijo que quería poner "escaleras" en la casa. 15

Blaine wanted to make knobs on the doors. He choose red paper.

Blaine decidió hacer un tirador para la puerta. Escogió el color rojo.

Teamwork—Kyleigh and Mikayla worked together to cut the masking tape.

Kyleigh y Mikayla trabajaron juntas para corta la cinta.

16

Figure 7.1. (cont'd)

In both the morning and afternoon classes, the children wanted to paint their houses.

En las dos clases, los niños decidieron pintar sus casas. 17

Meeting Pre-Kindergarten Goals

- Literacy
  La Lectura y Escritura

- Math
  Matemáticas

18

Mathematics / Matemáticas

- Begins to show an interest in numbers and quantity.
- *Tiene interés en los números y cantidad.*

Joshua wrote numbers 1, 2, 3, on his level.
Escribió 1, 2, 3 en el nivel.

Cooper added numbers to his level.
Cooper puso números en el nivel.
19

- Begins to compare sizes of objects

- *Empieza comparar los tamaños.*

"Alfombras grandes y chiquitas"
—*Fatima*

20

- Participates in measurement activities.

- *Participar en las actividades de medir.*

Ashton and Christopher worked together to measure boards for their "porch."

21

Literacy / La Lectura y Escritura

- Begins to see a purpose to writing.
- *Empieza a ver una razón para escribir.*

Blake wrote his mom a "message" on the thank you card.

Blake escribió un "mensaje" para su mamá en la carta de gracias.

22

- Identifies 10 letters, especially those in their names.
- *Identificar 10 letras, especialment las letras en su primer nombre.*

Arianna and Misael wrote their names on the thank you notes.

Arianna y Misael escribieron sus nombres en la carta de gracias.

23

We are learning how to learn!
¡Aprendimos como aprender!

24

presentation is longer and can contain more detailed information than could be covered in a newsletter or note home. The audience is parents, who are already a highly interested audience that perceives the information as relevant. With the presentation, this parent-night event is different from many open house type events in that parents will be sitting quietly and listening to the presentation in a coherent, focused way—not merely looking at a display while trying to entertain a temperamental young sibling at the same time. Even so, Ms. Wilson limited her presentation to a few bite-sized points and took care to make those points clearly and support them with evidence that is engaging, memorable, and fun. It is very likely that most parents will come away from the presentation with an understanding of Ms. Wilson's Project Approach teaching method and confidence that their children are progressing in their development of early math and literacy skills. This is the message she set out to communicate to them, so we can call this effective or successful strategic communication. While her presentation is aesthetically pleasing and enjoyable, what really makes it effective is the carefully chosen content. Throughout the rest of this chapter, we will take a closer look at how she strategically designed this communication to make it so effective.

Relevant Message

The first key to effective communication is choosing a relevant message. Audiences will only pay attention to messages that are relevant for them. Because there are so many communication channels and messages competing for their time, they must constantly scan and screen messages for relevance. Many messages will be dismissed as "not my problem." Personal relevance means that what the communicator has to say has some direct impact on the life of an audience member. This has two important implications for communicators.

First, there is little point in sharing things that aren't relevant. Communicators must choose just a few of the most important points to make. There is no point in wasting those few points on a message that will be ignored anyway. Of the many things you have to say, choose to focus on the ones your audience is most concerned about. Second, if the personal relevance isn't obvious to the audience, your message may be screened out even if it really was important. This means if the personal relevance isn't immediately obvious, the communicator will need to make that link for

the audience. For parents, their children are central to their lives, and almost anything related to their children seems personally relevant. Sometimes too much relevance may be an issue in communicating with parents. Some topics may be seen as pressing concerns for parents, and educators may need to address those concerns before parents can move on to other relevant topics. For other audiences, personal relevance is much less obvious.

There are numerous factors that can make a message seem personally relevant for someone:

- Direct or indirect gains, profit, or benefits for oneself or a party one represents (such as a company)
- Direct or indirect costs to oneself
- Direct impact on one's own life or the life of a loved one
- Connection to one's profession, hobby, or area of interest
- Connection to issues central to one's identity (e.g., a feminist perks up when the importance of female role models is mentioned)
- Expectation of making a decision or providing an opinion
- Expectation of taking some action
- Expectation that the information provided will be needed in the future
- Interacting or playing a role in the communication (such as answering a question)

Of course, this is not an exhaustive list; there are endless ways to help your audience feel personally involved in an issue. The key to choosing a message that is personally relevant is putting yourself in the audience's shoes and thinking about what they would find most interesting. Strategy One, "Analyze Your Audience," discussed perspectives for key audiences, which should help educators identify relevant messages.

At the parent-night event on the House Project, Ms. Wilson was fortunate to be facing an audience that was already highly interested and motivated. The personal relevance of her message was already clear to the parent audience. But the preschoolers learned hundreds of skills in the House Project, and Ms. Wilson had dozens of other examples she might have shared. She chose these three main points to emphasize: background information on the Project Approach, meeting math goals through the House Project, and meeting literacy goals through the House Project. Relevance to the audience, or audience needs, was the primary consideration for Ms. Wilson when she made those choices.

"It was the first project I had done with these families," she said, "so the first half [of the presentation] was to educate them on the Project Approach."

One reason to share this background information is simply because the audience does not know this information already and needs an understanding of the teaching method before they can easily make sense of the project. Another reason it is worth investing time and energy in this background information is that she will be working with this audience repeatedly over the whole year and will build on this knowledge later.

The decision to emphasize math and literacy goals was also driven primarily by audience needs. "I have found that parents really like to see the math and the literacy," she said. "Parents of prereaders are especially concerned about reading."

Because of her preschoolers' parents' concern about their children's ability to recognize numbers and letters and get ready for reading, Ms. Wilson said she always focuses on math and literacy. Other learning goals are discussed whenever a project seems well suited to showcasing them. In this case, the audience had three immediate needs: background information on the Project Approach and literacy and math goals. In order to have time to provide enough detail and support to meet those needs effectively, Ms. Wilson did not feel there was room to raise other issues. Once the background information has been covered, she can bring up other learning goals as she sees fit in future communications with this parent group.

Tight Focus

The second key to effective strategic communication is keeping a very tight focus on those few messages you really want to get across to your audience. Less is more. It is important to be realistic about the attention and effort your audience is willing to invest in your message as well as the amount of information they are likely to absorb. It is hard to underestimate this—the audience is likely to be less motivated and less energetic and will remember less than you think! Furthermore, the communicator is always more familiar with the information than the audience. This means that what seems simple and clear to the communicator appears more complex for the audience. The audience will have to work harder than the communicator to digest the message.

Like many forms of evidence, documentation of children's work serves multiple purposes, as discussed in Chapter 1. In the role of an educator, you may have collected extensive quantities of documentation of children's work for the purpose of guiding instruction, assessing children, and/or studying pedagogy. As a communicator, you are using documentation for a different purpose, that of achieving your communication goals. A key part of your role as a communicator is to serve as an expert gatekeeper or editor. Your audience is counting on you to know the whole story—but to select only the most important parts to share and to present those few important parts in a way that has meaning. However excited you as an educator may be about each piece of documentation, you cannot perform your role as an effective communicator unless you share selectively.

Professional communicators regularly perform the gatekeeper role, and journalists have it down to a science. For example, consider newspaper coverage of a fire at a local apartment building. A reporter and a photographer go to the scene of the fire and spend half a day there shooting photos and talking to people. They come away with lots of exciting quotes and photos. When readers look at the front page of the newspaper the next day, they don't see 20 photographs organized in rows and a story in chronological order quoting the landlord, firefighters, and 25 apartment residents. Why not? Wouldn't readers rather have more photos and more information? Don't they want the whole story? The answer is no. Readers do not want the whole story; they want meaning and a sense of involvement. The newsroom staff understands that need. Most likely, one dramatic and engaging photo is selected and printed large enough that it dominates the layout; possibly two or three additional photos are included. The dominant photo captures the bright color of the fire and the emotion in a close-up of a human face and is large enough to draw attention when, from a distance, someone sees the newspaper at a newsstand. People will be so drawn to that photo and attention-getting headline that they will pay to read the story. This would not happen if all 20 photographs were printed.

Furthermore, the reporter will organize the story with an emphasis on showing personal relevance and providing meaning. The basic information readers want to know about the fire is printed first: who, what, when, and where. Readers want to know how much damage was done and whether anyone was hurt. The most important fact discovered in the investigation is that the apartment building did not comply with the city fire code and that it had not been inspected in some time. This has implications for all apartment tenants in the city because their apartments might also be in violation of the code. The story provides the most important information up front and emphasizes the code violation, which is personally relevant for many readers. Many quotes and details are left out of the story so that readers can easily identify the key information. Readers value this gatekeeper function enough to pay for it.

When educator-communicators share documentation, they need to follow the example of journalists by being very selective about the points made and the evidence provided and keeping a tight focus on the messages they are trying to convey. Keeping a tight focus is important because of the following:

- *A selective, tightly focused communication piece is inviting rather than overwhelming.* This means more people will read or listen! If there is too much information, people can see at a glance that they will have to make an effort to sift out the important messages. An overwhelming communication piece looks like work to the audience, not meaning and information.

- *A selective, tightly focused piece can have large images and large type.* Large images draw people in. Type, photos, and images simply cannot be very large if there is too much packed into a display, newsletter, or other communication piece. Large images can be powerful enough to attract attention from across a room, especially close-ups of faces.

- *A tightly focused message can be absorbed even incidentally.* If the meaning is very clear and print and photos are large, people can pick up the essence of the message when scanning their environment, even if they do not decide it is worthy of further attention. For example, imagine a display in the lobby of a house of worship placed by a sponsored preschool to show how the program teaches religious values at an early age. Some members will pause to read the display on their way to a service, and some will merely pass by it afterwards on their way to the coffee hour. If the point is clear and the photos and type are large, those passers-by may very well absorb the idea that the preschool is part of their mission—and remember that later when it is time to allocate funding.

- *People can recall only about two to four points anyway.* It makes sense to use communication space or time to fully support those two to four points, making them as convincing, attention-getting, and memorable as possible. As discussed in Strategy Three, "Convince with Evidence,"

documentation is uniquely suited to be convincing, engaging, and memorable, but it needs space for depth, context, and explanation to make the meaning pop out for the audience.

Each of these reasons for keeping communication tightly focused is based on a realistic assessment of the audience's attention, motivation, and memory. The message needs to attract and invite audience attention, reach audience members who will pay minimal attention, and provide attentive audience members with key points.

With her parent-night presentation about the House Project, Ms. Wilson did an excellent job of making the meaning of the project pop out for her parent audience. Imagine a movie camera panning the whole scene of the House Project. Through the window formed by the camera lens, the audience sees a lot of activity going on, but the meaning is unclear. By zooming in on one scene at a time, the distractions disappear, and the audience knows exactly what to focus on.

Ms. Wilson's explanation of the Project Approach focused on five ways in which children learn through the approach: formulating questions, drawing, observing demonstrations, investigating, and representing learning. This does not tell the whole story of the Project Approach teaching method. Instead, this summary captures what she identified as the most important information her West Liberty parents needed. Breaking it down into five bite-sized points is like adjusting the focus to define an object of interest for the camera. It serves the purpose of making the relevant meaning pop out for the parent audience.

Actually, this five-point summary was not developed just for the parent night on the House Project. Ms. Wilson developed this simple five-point summary a few years ago. Since it worked well with that parent audience, she now uses it regularly to introduce new groups of families to the Project Approach. She customizes the questions, drawings, and examples for each project, but the five points remain the same, whether she prepares a documentation display, newsletter, or presentation. The five-point summary has become a sort of template. Her explanation probably gets better every time she uses it. Professional communicators frequently reuse summaries in this way.

Ms. Wilson also defined specific supporting points to communicate her main points that math and literacy goals were met through the project by specifying two or three skills for each. For math goals, she showed examples of children showing interest in num-

Plate 1. Documentation displays like this one show the value of teaching methods by capturing thinking processes such as problem solving and dispositions such as persistence in learning. These are meaningful outcomes that are not communicated through test scores but are valued by the public.

Can Project Work Change A Child's Learning Disposition?

After returning from the farm, a small group of children became interested in constructing the farm, the grain bins, and the fields of corn. One child, Stephen, became immersed in figuring out how to make the corn stand up in the block construction. Stephen's persistence was a huge change in his learning disposition!

Stephen first tried setting up the cornstalks on their own. They quickly fell down.

Next he tried to use putty to help them stand up, but that didn't work either.

Stephen then tried gluing them onto a plastic tray, and that worked!

Once the farm construction was finished, lots of dramatic play happened.

Using the Work Sampling Checklist, we could assess many different areas of the children's development.

It was so exciting watching Stephen engage in problem solving. It was a new behavior for him and I was able to document his growth for his portfolio.

Plate 2. This display for a toddler center helped to communicate to parents the value of early learning experiences for young children and increased the credibility of the center staff.

Can Toddlers Cooperate?

Project work provides opportunities for children to develop social skills.

"Toddlers are very concerned with their own needs and ideas. This is why we cannot expect them to share."

—National Network for Child Care

Interest in the vacuum cleaner begins.

Toddlers between the ages of 18 and 36 months are eager learners. They want to experience and know about everything! They are also developing confidence in their own abilities and learning how to communicate their needs and what they want to know about. When toddlers are involved in project work, this intense interest and curiosity often motivates them to cooperate with others to find solutions to problems. In this way, they develop social skills of listening to others and working together.

Look what happened when these toddlers explored the vacuum cleaner!

They learn that some objects will go through the tubes.

Then these boys discovered that, when cooperating as a team, they can "work" the clothespin from one end of the tube to the other by lifting parts in sequence. One child could not do the task alone. This task required each of them to do their part and to do it at the appropriate time.

Curiosity Corner, Northminster Learning Center, 2003–2004, Beth Jones, Teacher

Plate 3. After studying documentation, art teacher Pat Fontroy began to use documentation that included displays of student artwork in her school. By providing information about how and what children were learning, she increased interest in the children's work.

6TH Grade students create

O-o-o-ouch

FACE MASKS

 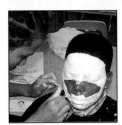 

Students paired off to create Paris craft masks on each others faces.
Models first had to prepare their faces using vaseline as a release agent and shower caps to protect their hair.

 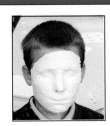

Left, student has mask applied with eyes open, and on the right, the student chooses to have his entire face covered, eyes included.

After the masks come off students reinforce edges and weak spots with more Paris craft saturated in white glue.
Students then sand rough surfaces and edges before designing the mask.

  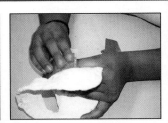

Students plan their final design on paper, then transfer the design directly onto the mask.
Painting the mask comes next as well as adding embellishments and dimensional designs.

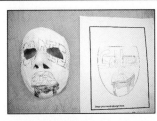

Plate 4. After learning about documentation, the staff of the Chicago Children's Museum began to document what children were learning not only in their museum visit but in their pre- and post-visit experiences. The 2004–2005 Student Visit Guide incorporated evidence of children's learning to show teachers the value of the museum experience.

Facilitated **Workshops**

Scholastic's The Magic School Bus Kicks Up a Storm™
Grades 1 – 5

Join Ms. Frizzle and her class, as you discover the wonders of weather within this playful, interactive environment. Learn about the science behind meteorology, the effects of climate on culture, and safety precautions for severe weather events. Your students will become weather detectives, using real tools to unravel the mysteries of the current weather conditions outside.

Presenting Sponsor: Sara Lee Foundation

Available March 1 - June 9, 2005
Tuesdays and Thursdays only.

Secrets of Painting
Grades 1 – 5

Unlock the secrets of painting with a visit to our working art studio. This workshop gives students a first-hand understanding of artist tools, techniques and the concepts of line and color, through a series of investigative activities about basic art elements. Students will apply these new-found discoveries, as they create unique works of art that can be hung in the classroom.

We can only accommodate one group per day.
Available Tuesdays, Wednesdays, and Fridays.

Treehouse Trails
Age 3 – Kindergarten

Discover the "great outdoors" in *Treehouse Trails*, an exhibit offering unlimited opportunities for pretend play in a realistic forest setting. In the *Treehouse Trails* workshop, students will learn about nature by exploring animal habitats and the natural landscape in a sensory-rich environment. Available Thursdays only.

WaterWays
Grades 1 – 5

This "splashy" exhibit allows students to pump, squirt and manipulate water, while learning about the multi-functional uses of this life-sustaining substance. In the team-based *WaterWays* workshop, students design an aqueduct system to gain first-hand knowledge of how water is moved from one place to another and the importance of harnessing its power to accomplish a multitude of functions.

How can first-graders become engaged in literacy?

The Dawes School teacher selects a topic familiar to all students—a backyard. Students web their ideas three times throughout the unit.

Then, the teacher integrates fantasy into the backyard unit by reading adventure books to the class.

Next, students embark on a fantasy adventure of their own in CCM's *BIG Backyard* workshop, where they become the main characters in a story.

Key:
Green=Time 1, Red=Time 2, Black=Time 3

Plate 4. (cont'd)

Facilitated Workshop **Information**

Allowable group size, cost per child and workshop schedules are based on the age of your group. Before submitting your reservation, please refer to the information below.

	Workshops for Age 3 through Kindergarten	**Workshops for Grades 1 – 5**
Cost	$4.00 per child	$5.00 per child
Group Size	A minimum of 15 and a maximum of 20 children, plus 1 adult for every 5 students *If your kindergarten class has more than 20 students, please call 312-464-7670 to make special arrangements.* *To ensure a quality experience for young children, we are following the National Association for the Education of Young Children's recommendation for group size.*	A minimum of 15 and a maximum of 35 children, plus 1 adult for every 5 students
# of Groups	2 concurrent groups for each workshop, unless noted	2 concurrent groups for each workshop, unless noted
Available	October 1- June 10, Tuesday-Friday, unless noted	October 1- June 10, Tuesday-Friday, unless noted
Time	Workshop: 10–11:30am Museum exploration not included	Workshop: 10–11:30am, Museum exploration: 11:30am–12:15pm

It begins in their own backyard!

See *BIG Backyard* workshop description on page 4.

Afterward, the students collaborate to create a BIG book that captures their experiences.

The orange group got to put bug costumes on. We pretended we were bugs and went digging for the book. We found the book !

If I were as small as a bee in my backyard I would fly up in my tree when it whould rain.

Finally, students build on literacy skills developed in the BIG Backyard unit, writing fantasy stories about their own backyards.

Teacher reflection

The children grew and expanded upon their reading, language, and writing skills throughout the backyard project. They discussed the various items found in their backyards with other students as they worked on the literacy activities. This led to greater acquisition of language, literacy, and speaking skills, particularly for my ESL students. The students had so much fun with all of the backyard activities in the classroom and at CCM that they didn't even realize they were meeting the first grade standards for language arts! Learning was so much fun for all of us.

Jean Rowe, Dawes School

6

Plate 5. This series illustrates how arrangement of photos and text can distract the viewer from focusing on children and their work and from being drawn into reading additional information about the experience.

Literacy skills are often taught and practiced during our center time. Children teach and encourage their friends.

a.

This is Fun!

Literacy skills are often taught and practiced during our center time. Children teach and encourage their friends.

b.

Literacy skills are often taught and practiced during our center time. Children teach and encourage their friends.

c.

Literacy skills are often taught and practiced during our center time. Children teach and encourage their friends.

d.

Literacy skills are often taught and practiced during our center time. Children teach and encourage their friends.

e.

Literacy skills are often taught and practiced during our center time. Children teach and encourage their friends.

f.

Plate 6. Series of display shots.

Our Corn Project

See how much fun we all had!

6a. This typical bulletin board display of photos and headlines tells little about the actual experience and emphasizes fun rather than learning.

What do children learn when they study corn?

XXXX XXXX XX X
XXXXX XXX XXXXX
XXXXX XX XXX XXX

XXXX XXX XXXXXX XXXXX XXX
XX XXXXXXX XXX XX XXXXXXX
XXX XX XXXX X

XX XXXXXX X XXXXXX XX

XXXX XXX XXXXXX
XXXXX XXX XX XXXX
XXX XXX XX XXXXXXX XXX
XX XXXX X

XXX XXXXXX XXXXX X XXXXX XX XXX

XXXXX XX XXXXXXX XXXXXXX X XXX
XXXXX XXXXX XXX XXXXX XX XXX

Science, reading, and problem solving!

6b. The display is improved by adding a new title and subtitle that are focused on learning and that ask and answer a question, by including captions to explain the photos and work (captions are shown here as XXXs for the purpose of discussing display), by using contrasting fonts in the title and subtitle, by varying the sizes of the photos, and by showing samples of children's work.

Plate 6. (cont'd)

What do children learn when they study corn?

XXXX XXXX XX X
XXXXX XXX XXXXX
XXXXX XX XXX XXX

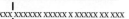
XXXX XXX XXXXXX XXXXX XXX
XX XXXXXXX XXX XX XXXXXXX
XXX XX XXXX X

XX XXXXXX X XXXXXX XX

XXXX XXX XXXXXX
XXXXX XXX XX XXXX
XXX XXX XX XXXXXX XX XXX
XX XXXX X

XXX XXXXX XXXX X XXXXX XX XXX

XXXXX XX XXXXXXX XXXXXXX X XXX
XXXXX XXXXX XXX XXXXX XX XXX

Science, reading, and problem solving!

6c. The display is checked for alignment. Alignment can make the display pleasing to look at and absorb. On this display, photos, captions, and titles do not line up—the display does not conform to the invisible lines (shown here with dashed lines) that the viewer draws with his or her eyes.

What do children learn when they study corn?

XXXX XXX XXXXXX XXXXX XXX
XX XXXXXXX XXX XX XXXXXXX
XXX XX XXXX X

XXXXX XXX XXXXX XXXX

XXX XXXXXX XXXXX X XXXXX XX XXX

XX XXXXXX X XXXXXX XX

XXXXX XX XXXXXXX XXXXXXX X XXX
XXXXX XXXXX XXX XXXXX XX XXX

XXXX XXXX XX XXXXX XXX XXXXX XX

XXXX XXXXX XXX XX XXX

Could it be science ... reading and writing ... and problem solving?

6d. The photos and titles are now aligned. The photos, work samples, and captions are placed in three columns to provide a sense of repetition. Captions are placed immediately next to the photos or work samples (proximity). The panel appears easy to read and understand. Changing the subtitle to a question at the bottom of the page encourages viewers to make a decision, thereby increasing interest and the probability that the display will be remembered.

bers, comparing sizes of objects, and participating in measurement activities. For literacy goals, she showed examples of children learning about the purpose of writing and how to identify letters. For each of these supporting points, one or two examples of children's work were selected. Because her experience in working with parents of preschoolers has shown her that her audience is very concerned about children recognizing numbers and letters, she always includes those supporting points. The examples chosen for sharing are the ones that most convincingly make the point, that is, the examples in which it is most clear that children are recognizing numbers and letters.

The other supporting points are chosen based on the best documentation available. "I look for examples where you can really see what they're thinking; where you can really see that they understand and take it one step further." The measurement example she shared from the House Project showed this. Two of the children decided to work together to measure boards for their porch. At first, they were pretending to use a tape measure and not really measuring, but then they started to use blocks as measuring tools. They realized that one long block was the same length as two short blocks. Ms. Wilson chose to share this because it clearly showed the thought process and demonstrated higher-level thinking. It was also engaging evidence because the audience can be drawn into the story of the children's discovery.

One way to bring your message into focus is to carefully define and specify it, breaking it down into identifiable points and supporting points. Another key to keeping a tight focus on your message is to eliminate distractions. After you've finished your first draft of your communication piece, do one more quick check to be certain that everything included supports your points. Anything off-message should be eliminated.

One of the reasons Ms. Wilson's PowerPoint presentation is so effective is that it contains no information or examples that are not directly tied into the points she was trying to communicate. This probably means she had a lot of interesting documentation she did not get to share! But by keeping this tight focus, her audience will come away convinced and will remember her message.

STRUCTURING YOUR MESSAGE: THE INVERTED PYRAMID

Professional communicators are well aware that audience members may lose interest at any time. Because of this, communicators must constantly persuade the audience to keep paying attention and try to get the most important information across as soon as possible. If the audience drifts away early, they will take with them only the portion of the message delivered up to that point. For these reasons, journalists have mastered a technique known as "inverted pyramid style."

As Figure 7.2 shows, the width of the pyramid represents the importance of information and its height represents the order in which it should be presented in the story. Think back to the news story about the local apartment fire. Chronological order would be easy to understand for readers who read the whole story, but readers who did not finish the story would be missing the most important information. The beginning of the story also is probably not the most exciting part, so readers would not be very enticed to read further either.

With the inverted pyramid, the headline usually summarizes the most exciting conclusion from the story. Next, newspaper journalists try to pack the most critical information for their readers, the famous "W's" (who, what, when, where, and maybe how and why), into the first paragraph or even the first sentence of the story, called the "lead." Based on that, readers can decide whether to continue the story or not. The second paragraph adds the next most important details and so on. The least important information is provided at the end of the story, because only the most interested readers will get this far. In fact, newspaper editors, in their gatekeeper role, may cut this story to fit available space. Knowing the end of the story contains the least important information, editors can simply chop off the last paragraphs.

Figure 7.2. Inverted pyramid diagram.

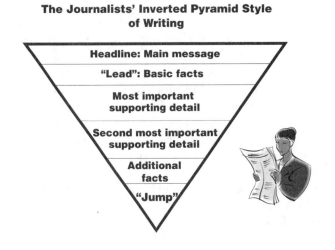

This organizational pattern is helpful to the audience. It helps them quickly obtain the important information and decide whether the story is relevant enough to warrant continued reading. The inverted pyramid organizational pattern is also helpful to the communicator. The communicator accepts that not everyone will continue reading or listening and plans for it. Even if readers only read the first paragraph, the most essential point has been made. Often, even a quick scan of the headline makes the point. Information is conveyed in priority order, getting the key message across even for unmotivated audience members.

Although newspaper journalism takes this approach to the extreme, most professionally designed communication follows this pattern. Museum displays, for example, use a hierarchical series of headings and subheadings. Some museum guests will move slowly through the entire museum, reading all the information, while others will move quickly through, skimming the headings and enjoying the artifacts. Well-designed headings and subheadings provide skimmers with the basic information while providing an organizing framework to guide the detail-readers. An effective exhibit works for museum guests who have only an hour to see the highlights, while still providing a full experience for guests who can dedicate a whole day.

OFFERING ADDITIONAL INFORMATION: THE JUMP

One way to relieve the pain of not sharing that great documentation you've collected is to offer it as additional, optional information.

Think back to our example of the newspaper staff covering the local apartment fire. One of us (Amanda), in her experience as newspaper reporter, actually covered a similar apartment fire. It was big news for a small town, and the fire photographs were among the most exciting seen in months. Choosing just one for the front page and leaving out all those other great shots was hard. In the end, the decision was made to provide a photo page deeper in the newspaper. Although the communicator's own excitement about the photos was a big part of the motivation for the photo page, it was also effective communication. The dominant front-page photo attracted readers' attention and drew them in. Once readers were engaged in the story, some of them would be interested enough to continue on to the page full of photos. Of course, others would not bother, but because the front page was selective and focused, those readers would not be

discouraged by an overwhelming layout either. The photo page was an extra bonus for the most interested readers.

In fact, newspapers and magazines often use a similar approach with text as well. An important story may begin on the front page, with the headline, perhaps a subhead, and the first few paragraphs or most important part of the story on that front page. Then the story continues (or, in newspaper lingo, "jumps") to another page inside the newspaper. Often newspapers and magazines have a "jump page" that contains primarily the continuations of many stories. Magazines likewise use an attention-getting, engaging first page and then hope the reader will be sufficiently engaged in the story to make the jump. Jump pages are usually designed very differently from front pages—they look plain and are designed to accommodate as much text as possible. Because readers who make the jump are already hooked on the story, jump pages are not designed to attract attention.

Additional information is also offered in boxes or sidebars, and design techniques are used to signal that these are optional reading even when they appear on the first page of a story. Enticing boxes and sidebars keep the main story from being overwhelming and give the reader a sense of being invited to explore. They also give designers a way to make blocks of text more visually appealing.

Other professional communicators follow the same idea in different ways. At the simplest level, audiences are given the opportunity to ask questions. Museum displays offer the most critical and engaging information on the display but invite museum guests to open drawers for additional exhibits, flip through photo albums, or explore additional reading material in an archive room or reading room. Broadcast media offer additional information on their websites. Public relations practitioners put the core message in a press release but include background information and additional materials in a folder known as a "press kit." Because the main press release is very short and to the point, reporters can quickly spot the most important news but still have a library of information to draw on if they want more depth. On websites, viewers are invited to click for background information or for more details. One of the great strengths of the Internet is that viewers can easily control exactly how much information and what information they see. This allows communicators to provide extensive details via layers of links, providing all the information anyone could want without overwhelming anyone.

Educators can likewise offer their audiences some kind of "jump page." A panel display can highlight just a few meaningful examples of documentation, but other examples of children's work can be displayed on classroom walls—unobtrusive but still available. A project history book can be set out during a parent-night event or sent home to families one at a time. A hall display might show one example project enlarged and labeled to help audiences grasp its significance but include all the children's work around it. A website can offer details and background—in fact, standard web pages with background information about teaching methodologies and state standards can be left online all the time, and this enriching extra information can be connected to any new pages with a link. Brochures with background information on teaching methodologies, center mission statement or philosophy, district curriculum goals, and so forth can be set out during any event. Individual portfolios can be shared with each child's parents.

After audience members have been drawn in and have begun to find meaning in a communication piece, at least some of them may be ready for more. They may even feel enthusiastic enough to seek out more information and ask questions, whereas they would have tuned out the whole thing if they had initially felt overwhelmed. You will probably find that audiences will spend more time meaningfully thinking about documentation when the initial display is minimal and tightly focused on attracting attention and making meaning. Not only does this approach "hook" the audience, but it also provides a framework of meaning so that the audience can make sense of additional information. The additional information is thus more appealing than it would have been if the whole package had been displayed from the start—and more meaningful to the audience as well.

SEEING THE BIG PICTURE

An educational professional can improve the effectiveness of communications simply by increasing the relevance and focus and using a structure such as the inverted pyramid. However, no communication event stands alone. Educator-communicators can take strategic communication to an even higher level by looking at the bigger picture and setting long-term goals for all communication. Just as professional communicators consider a campaign, teachers might consider all of their communications with parents for the school year.

Professional communicators, such as public relations practitioners, political campaign planners, and advertising copywriters, often spend a considerable portion of their planning time articulating and specifying communication goals or objectives in terms of the desired audience response. They use a format similar to this:

> After my [speech, meeting, display, newsletter], [audience] will [action or thinking].

The latter part of the statement specifies who the intended audience is and what response is desired. In this case, the first part of the statement specifies a particular upcoming communication event that is being planned. Of course, we don't always carefully articulate goals before beginning, and sometimes the goals are obvious. But if you cannot make this kind of statement, your communication is unlikely to be effective. Making this simple statement, even just as a quick mental check, serves as a good reminder of what you are trying to communicate.

The next sections provide questions to help identify those goals.

Goal: Developing Understanding

What do you want the audience to think? The answer to this question will result in communication goals that focus on having the audience develop knowledge, understanding, and attitudes. Educators may want parents to understand their child's progress or to understand why the school uses a particular methodological approach. In answering this question, communicators need to push beyond situation-specific facts to underlying communication goals. Why is it important to communicate this news to this audience?

There are two aspects of the audience's perspective to consider here. Besides asking yourself what you want the audience to think (or know or understand), as a communicator you should also ask yourself, "What does the audience want or need to know or understand?" Often the answers to these two questions are one and the same, but if they're not, you may need to communicate more than one message—both what you want them to know and what they want to know.

Imagine that a school district has added a new public preschool program. The teacher wants his audience of school board members to understand that the children's early literacy work in his classroom contributes to children's mastery of reading later. The school board wants to know that children are reading in pre-school, which is unrealistic for this group of children. These two issues are very close but are not identical. The teacher needs to recognize that the school board is focused on actual reading. He can communicate what he wants to say about his students' prereading activities, but he needs to make sure his message also provides the answer to the question in school board members' minds. This means the link between the pre-reading behaviors and actual reading should probably be explicitly addressed in the message, which could be as simple as adding a single sentence stating that recognizing that print has meaning and associating letters with sounds are first steps in the process of learning to read. This link may be so obvious for the teacher that he is entirely focused on achieving those prereading steps, but viewing the question from the audience's perspective can help him make his message more effective for that audience.

The second audience consideration to keep in mind here is that what you want the audience to think is dependent on what the audience already does think. What do they already know or believe? Are there misconceptions you want to correct? Is there background information that you need to provide? In our school board example above, perhaps district achievement scores have recently shown students are below average in reading and the district is campaigning to improve reading at all levels. This tells the teacher that school board members are probably already thinking about reading in their district. They perceive reading as a problem for their district and are motivated to solve it.

Sometimes this line of questioning tells the communicator as much about him- or herself as it does about the audience—your answer to the question "What does the audience already think?" is really your perception or presumption about what the audience thinks. Perhaps our new preschool teacher is assuming that, unaccustomed to considering the needs of pre-schoolers, the board has unrealistic expectations about the kind of activities his students should be doing. This may very well be true! But it may not be true, or it may be true only for some of the board members. He can most effectively communicate his ideas to board members from either perspective, as long as the presentation or display doesn't give board members the feeling that the teacher assumes they have the wrong idea about what is developmentally appropriate for children. He can make the same point but should be careful about projecting the assumption that his audi-

ence has the wrong idea. Remember the communication model—even when someone tries to tell us exactly what he or she thinks, the message must be encoded by the communicator and decoded by the listener. We can never really know what the audience thinks. But checking our assumptions and consciously considering the audience's perspective can help us come much closer than we would if we left that aspect of the communication process on automatic.

Goal: Building Relationships

What do you want your relationship with the audience to be? Sometimes the audience attitudes or beliefs are about the relationship between the educator and the audience—a teacher wants parents to feel that he respects them; a principal wants teachers to feel that she sympathizes with their concerns about budget cuts. Messages about the relationship between the audience and the communicator, called relational messages, are always being sent, whether the communicator intends to send them or not. Frequently, they are not explicitly stated, but the audience members consciously or unconsciously look for cues that signal the communicator's attitude toward them. These cues are typically conveyed in the way a message is phrased and by nonverbal signals such as eye contact, gestures, and facial expression. People tend to be much more aware of the relational messages they receive than they are of the ones they send. We actively try to "read" people, but we often pay little attention to the signals we are sending, unknowingly giving the audience the impression that we don't care much, or don't understand their perspective, or don't respect them.

Particularly because of the importance of the communicator–audience relationship in establishing credibility, relational messages can be important communication goals. Although these messages will probably not be explicitly stated, they are much more likely to be conveyed if the communicator consciously acknowledges them as communication goals. Building credibility should always be a communication goal. As discussed in Strategy Two, "Invest in the Most Credible Communicators," credibility consists of both expertise and trustworthiness, and liking and respect for the audience are major factors in establishing trustworthiness. In addition, educators may consider other relational message goals for particular situations, such as showing appreciation for parents or field trip hosts. It is a good idea to include relational messages on your list of communication goals.

In our example with Ms. Wilson's house-building project, she has an ongoing goal to encourage parent involvement. With this in mind, she selected documentation examples that emphasized the role of a father in the project. He came to the class and demonstrated building a wall, actually building a small bit of wall right there in the classroom. Including him in the photos showed appreciation and acknowledgement of his contribution.

"It was a way of thanking him," Ms. Wilson said.

Not only does the acknowledgement make this particular father feel good, it also sends a message to other parents that such contributions are appreciated and valued.

Goal: Motivating Action

What do you want your audience to do? Action goals are difficult to achieve because your audience members must be very motivated to actually get up and do something. Communication research shows that action goals are more likely to be achieved if the call to action is explicitly stated. That's why so many commercials conclude with seemingly obvious statements like "Buy now" or "Ask your doctor for more information." In some cases in the education context, action goals are the primary purpose of communication—the goal is to get permission slips signed and returned or to have parents sign up for parent–teacher conferences. In those cases, educators are already quite accustomed to strategically making that call to action very explicit: "Sign your name on the dotted line and have your child return the signed permission slip by Friday or your child will not be able to go on the field trip to the apple orchard." Not only is the call to action explicit, but another strategic communication technique is used as well: Consequences of the lack of action are specifically stated as an additional incentive to motivate the desired behavior.

Often, in education-related communications, the primary goal is developing understanding or building relationships, and action goals are not so obvious to the communicator or the audience. There are many missed opportunities for educator-communicators to get more from their partners in the educational process—audiences both inside and outside the school. As you are choosing your messages, ask yourself if there are actions you would like the audience to take. You may have action goals you have not even explicitly stated to yourself. One step to accomplishing those goals is recognizing them in your own mind so that you can strategically design communication to accomplish them.

State Your Call to Action

The next step is to consider explicitly stating a call to action. Sometimes all you have to do is ask! Calls to action can be made even stronger by linking them to consequences. For example, a parent newsletter with news about the class project is valuable as is. But adding a call to action would make it stronger. There could simply be a box with a few bullet points on "Ways You Can Help with Our Bee Study"—collect egg cartons for building our hive, bring in any books on bees or bugs, talk about bees with your child at home, volunteer for our field trip to the bee farm. Adding a mention of the positive consequences could make this communication stronger yet, such as one sentence stating "Continuing their exploration at home will reinforce learning and build children's enthusiasm for our investigation." Then a list of questions to ask and vocabulary terms to use could be provided.

Of course, explicit calls to action are not always appropriate and can seem "pushy." But all too often the communicator, who already knows exactly what he or she is thinking, imagines that the need for action is clearer than it is. Being overly concerned about being too pushy can mean your audience members may never make the connection between your message and their behavior. Educators deal with many audiences who are predisposed to help, such as parents, school boards, and principals. An explicit call to action may simply provide the audience with useful information or guidance by telling them how they can help.

In our newsletter example above, it is certainly true that many parents would talk about the bee project at home without being told. But there also may be parents who want to encourage their children in school but don't really know how. While they might have asked their children about the school project, it might not have occurred to them to also study bees at home with the children or to make a conscious effort to emphasize vocabulary terms. Even those parents who would have talked with their children about bees anyway may feel more involved in the project when they see that behavior on the list of ways they can support the project. Calls to action can come in the form of hints, suggestions, tips, or recommendations, as well as commands.

Another reason for explicitly stating a call to action is that it shifts the audience's perspective to a higher level of personal involvement. An audience member who is *considering taking an action* is more motivated to pay attention to a message than one who is merely listening with no expectation of acting. When we know we can do something, we are naturally more interested. This means that even for people who don't end up taking any action, an explicit call to action may increase their attention level. This can be especially important when reaching out to audiences whose involvement with the school or center is more distant, such as taxpayers without children of their own. Recommending actions they can take reminds them that they can play a role and that they have a reason to pay attention to the issue. In short, it can be a way to establish personal relevance.

Summing Up

In an ideal world, educators would set aside some time on a regular basis to actually generate a list of important messages or communication goals for key audiences, based on answering these key questions:

1. What do you want the audience to think?
2. What do you want your relationship with the audience to be?
3. What do you want the audience to do?

Even with limited time, educators can use these questions as a quick check to get more out of the communication they are already doing. Establishing goals early in the process of drafting a newsletter or press release, writing a note home, or organizing an open house can make your communication much more efficient and effective. Try to get into the habit of following these three steps:

1. Simply take a moment to articulate your goal for yourself, perhaps in the form of the desired audience response—"After reading my newsletter, parents will be informed of our progress on the bee project and will understand how literacy goals are being met through the project."
2. Then ask yourself "Could I get more out of this communication?" and consider the three communication goals: developing understanding, building relationships, and motivating action.
3. Then, before you hit the print button, do one more quick check: Does this communication accomplish what you intended? Is the audience likely to respond in the right way? Are the relational messages the ones you intended to send?

PLANNING A MESSAGE CALENDAR

Another way to take a broader view of your communication with an audience you will be communicating with regularly is to look at the series of communications as a whole. Plan a series of bite-sized points that will combine over time to deliver your whole message. For example, rather than discussing all curriculum goals at once, plan to emphasize one or two in each monthly newsletter.

Professional communicators such as public relations practitioners and political campaign directors often use a message calendar to schedule when messages will be delivered. This allows the campaign planners to ensure that all the messages will eventually be delivered and to plan the best times to deliver each message. For example, the winter holidays are probably not the best time to try to deliver a complex message. Political campaign planners often time statements on veterans' issues with Veteran's Day or Memorial Day or statements on education issues with back-to-school times. Educators might schedule discussion of assessment issues to coincide with the annual release of standardized test results or plan to discuss physical development curriculum goals when there are annual physical fitness contests.

A teacher or principal might plan a "message calendar" for the school year by noting major school dates, school board meetings, and relevant political events such as a tax vote, and pencil in likely communications such as a monthly newsletter. Message topics can be penciled in with consideration for the time of year, competing school news events, and likely available documentation. A message calendar template is provided in Chapter 11, Foundation Builders.

A teacher might plan to cover personal/social goals early in the year when parents are most concerned about children adjusting to a new classroom or new school, and cover science goals later in the school year, when children's science and investigative skills have developed enough to produce exciting documentation examples. Of course, if excellent documentation comes in that would support a particular point, a message calendar can be adjusted at any time.

A less formal approach would be to make a list at the start of the school year of key messages to deliver. For each newsletter or each parent night, a teacher or principal could simply look at the list for ideas, choose a few points to make based on available documentation, and cross those points off the list, leaving the rest for later communications. A teacher might use this approach to make sure all children are featured in the newsletter at least once (putting children's names on a message list); a principal might use this approach to make sure each grade level is featured.

Using some form of message calendar helps communicators to do the following:

- Ensure messages do not get overlooked
- Time messages for minimum competition and maximum impact
- Ensure that repeated coverage of topics reflects the importance of those topics
- Remind themselves to repeat important messages

Once communicators have delivered a message, they often make the mistake of assuming that because it has been said they do not need to say it again. This is not true. As educators know well, people often need to hear a message many times before they fully learn it. Professional communicators also know this—that's why we end up seeing the same annoying commercials so many times! Repetition helps memory.

But there are two other reasons it is a good idea to use the message calendar to remind yourself to repeat messages. The first is that there is no guarantee your entire audience got the message the first time. For example, consider a church preschool that places a display in the church lobby highlighting the link between the school and the church's religious mission. The preschool director may feel that message has been delivered. Yet there could be numerous church members who did not see it. Perhaps they attended that Sunday but entered through a different door or got distracted just as they passed the display. Or perhaps they skipped church that Sunday.

A second reason to repeat the message is that audiences change over time. In the church preschool example, within a few months or a year, some members have left the church and some new members have joined. Others may be the same individuals, but their perspective has changed. Perhaps at the time the first display was shown, a young woman saw it as irrelevant and paid little attention. Now she is expecting her first child and is planning for that child's education. Audiences also change because they gain knowledge and understanding and need time to adjust to new ideas. Many of us have had the experience of reading the same book again after time has passed and finding new meaning in the exact same words. Audiences focus on the part of the message that is most relevant to them; they take what they are ready for. Later, they may be ready for more. The church preschool in our example could use a message calendar to plan to remind church members of the role of the school in the church mission every 3 or 6 months.

Communicators themselves are very involved in their own issues—that's why they are qualified to speak out! They also hear the message every time they deliver it, to every audience. Audiences are much less involved, and particular audience members only hear a small fraction of the messages delivered. If you don't feel like you're saying the same thing over and over, there's a good chance your audience hasn't heard it enough.

BACK TO THE INVERTED PYRAMID

This chapter was written in inverted pyramid style, in case any of you readers skipped or skimmed the last sections. If it were in chronological order, setting communication goals would naturally be discussed first. Instead, the chapter is presented with what we thought was most important for you to remember and apply in case you got tired and skimmed the rest of the chapter. After seeing many educators' communications that lacked a relevant message and tight focus, we wanted to be sure that we got those two points across first. If readers of this book will take those just those two messages to heart, communication will be significantly improved! Thus, the chapter starts with the two keys to effective communication—relevant message and tight focus—and moves on to some specific strategies from professional communicators: inverted pyramid style, then a "jump" to information for those who are interested in a more detailed approach to communication, including writing explicit goals and message calendars.

CHAPTER 8

Strategy 5

Incorporate Evidence: Ways to Share Your Documentation

Once you have a clear understanding of what you want to communicate and how powerful documentation of student learning can be in accomplishing those goals, you will see many opportunities to use evidence of children's learning. This chapter discusses ways educator-communicators can incorporate documentation and strategic communication to maximize the power of communication channels they are already using. Some of the common channels used by schools and centers where documentation can be integrated are the following:

- School or center brochures
- District brochures or welcome packets
- Newsletters
- Web pages
- Notes home
- Community displays
- Open houses
- Hallway displays
- Books or project histories
- Portfolios or assessment folders on student performance
- Press releases
- Displays at locations in the community that students have studied

The opportunities for strategic use of children's work to broaden the perspective of others who interact with or view educational institutions from the outside are limited only by the imagination. Here are some examples of how this can be done.

DISPLAYS

Displays are more than bulletin boards. Most educators have had little training in display as a communication method. If the topic of display was introduced in their pre-service training, it was usually covered under the use of classroom bulletin boards that are intended for a student audience. Whenever displays are created in hallways in schools or other educational institutions, the educator must assume that these will be viewed by the public and that the public will be drawing conclusions about the institution and the learning experience based on the display. If a person walking into the entryway of a school sees only cartoon characters or banners proclaiming "Spring is fun time!" what conclusion might a visitor draw about what occurs there? If instead a person walks into an entryway where children's work is displayed in an aesthetically pleasing way, where learning goals are attached to children's work, where photos of children working are on the walls, where chairs or benches encourage visitors to linger and examine evidence of children's learning, and where the atmosphere is contemplative rather than carnival-like, what might the visitor conclude? And what messages might these approaches send to the school's primary audience, students?

The most obvious places for educator-communicators to create displays are in their own institutions. Besides these displays inside schools and centers, there are also many opportunities for displays in the community and at public events. Public places such as malls and airports frequently set aside display space for the use of schools and centers as a public service. Family restaurants and fast-food franchises frequently display children's work to encourage families to enter their facility to view the work. Educators, too, often tend to transfer concepts about bulletin boards to these communication displays with unfortunate results. They use what they think appeals to children such as cartoon or commercial art, bright borders, primary colors, or fonts that appear to be printed by a child. Some even include backwards letters or misspelled words in an attempt to give the impression of being childlike. This does not build credibility or enhance the professional standing of educators.

Displays as Opportunities

There is much that we can learn from museum professionals about how to use display space as a communication channel. Museum exhibit design research is especially meaningful to educators because of the similarities of the role of displays in museums. Viewers of public education displays, like viewers of museum exhibits, decide whether or not to stop and look, how long to stay, and how much effort to expend on thinking about the subject of the display. The experience is completely controlled by the viewer, unlike a bulletin board display in a classroom, where a captive audience spends extensive time. A consideration in designing displays for nonstudent viewers, then, is how to capture and keep their attention or, in museum terminology, "holding power" (Miles & Tout, 1990). Observations of individuals looking at displays in museums have revealed that even when displays are carefully designed and located and when viewers have come specifically for the purpose of seeing displays, they spend a very short amount of time looking at each display.

Incorporating Documentation

Incorporating documentation in displays inside educational institutions varies by location. Displays inside classrooms are primarily for children and are educational. Displays immediately outside classrooms are for children and others and are somewhat more public. Then there are the areas of schools and centers that are very public—entryways, areas where large meetings are held, or hallways where training is held. These more public areas where there is extensive traffic are where many educational institutions place "published documentation."

As defined in Chapter 1, published documentation is evidence of children's learning that has been carefully mounted with word-processed narrative and photos. The most powerful pieces have been strategically selected. Documentation inside classrooms is considered raw documentation and is used by the teacher and children during the process of learning experiences. Documentation immediately outside classrooms is somewhere between raw and published depending on how frequently it is viewed by parents and the general public. Display techniques that occur outside classrooms can be more strategic and effective without being so time-consuming or formal as documentation display panels. For example, a narrative explaining how a piece of work was created might be neatly printed and mounted next to the work in the hallway. One school provides each learning goal for the school on laminated strips available in the Teacher Center. A teacher who has put up a display in the hallway can simply go to the center, select the goals that were accomplished in the learning experience, and display them with the student work. Though not as formal as published documentation, this approach is certainly strategic, effective, and efficient.

Incorporating documentation into displays in the community can focus the community on what schools and centers do best (i.e., education) and evidence of that education (i.e., documentation). Some less-than-effective, but typical, displays that we viewed included the following:

- A display of children's artwork in a fast-food restaurant that lacked the ages of the children, how the work was done, what was learned, or what learning experience prompted the artwork.
- A high school display in a mall that had the name of the high school, three pieces of artwork, and four trophies. Three of the trophies were for athletic teams, with one accompanying team photo. One photo was of a scholastic competition. The viewer had to be motivated to look closely at the trophies and read the inscription to discover why they were awarded.
- Three displays in three different airports on the local school system. Two of these included large photos of the administrative office of the school district. One of the three had a photo of each school in the district. Another consisted totally of athletic trophies and photos. One display was obviously prepared by a public relations professional to provide information for prospective families.

All of the educators who designed these displays thought they were communicating about their program. They all required a time commitment, and some required considerable effort. How might documentation have enhanced these displays?

The fast-food art display could have been improved by providing a context for viewers—ages of the children, what inspired the work, what the children said, what they learned either about the technique used or the subject of the work. If the program had curriculum goals or standards related to this learning experience, these could have been displayed with the work. A more powerful exhibit might provide evidence of growth with samples of children's work over a period of time (time 1, time 2, time 3). Instead of work by all the children of the same learning experience (e.g., water painting), different kinds of art experiences could be displayed with labels of the kind of experience and benefits for learning. Viewers would then understand the comprehensiveness of the art experiences provided to students. Several photos of students working would enhance the display and encourage diners to linger and look. An effective poster, such as that in Color Plate 3, would explain how the artwork was done, how it tied in to standards, as well as capture the attention of the viewers.

The high school mall display would have worked better if the artwork included an explanation of the learning experience, age level, and so forth. Was this a freshman art experience provided to everyone? If so, what was learned? Or was this the award-winning artwork of a senior? If it was the latter, the display would have been enhanced by a photo of the artist and an explanation of how the high school provided specific opportunities for her to develop her skills in art and what she intended to do. The inclusion of trophies indicates that perhaps this display was meant to focus on excellence. If so, a heading such as "Students at Elmore High Are Honored for Outstanding Achievement" could be read quickly, even by those passing by and not stopping. The addition of photos and student comments about what they learned from being on an athletic team would emphasize the educational benefit of the experience. The scholastic trophy could also be enhanced with photos and narratives, with perhaps sample questions to challenge the viewer. Participating in this reflective process of display preparation would benefit the students as well.

As for the airport displays, it is unlikely that many viewers would find the photos of the administrative office interesting. Although prospective families may be viewing this display, there will also be visitors to the community, prospective business partners, current students and their families, and many taxpayers who are going in and out of the airport on business or pleasure trips. Evidence of student learning would enhance this display. Photos of school buildings or the administrative offices are unlikely to get across the most important message that the schools would like to get across: These schools are educating students; here is evidence of how we do it.

Some locations most often overlooked for community displays are places where students have studied or community businesses or organizations have supported learning experiences. For example, if a class has been studying veterinarians and has visited a veterinary clinic, the clinic would be a perfect place for a display of evidence of children's learning in the project. An effective display would focus on what children learned from the experience. It could include children's concepts about animals before the study contrasted with concepts after the study, a list of vocabulary words, samples of writing including a child-made book about the topic, a list of the ways veterinarians use math, or other examples that reflect student learning in a way that will be particularly interesting to clinic staff. Such a display need not be huge—a trifold equivalent of three poster boards would be sufficient—but the selection of documentation should be strategic.

The display could be placed in the clinic for several months, educating and entertaining waiting clients. Such a display would enhance the relationship between the school and the clinic and between the families and the clinic. It would also enhance the image of both the school and the clinic. Such displays are often welcome in libraries and other community locations such as senior citizen centers.

Since the needs of audiences not directly involved with the school are similar, the same display may be well suited for several community locations. It may be effective, as well as efficient, to design a single display that will work well for the clinic and for the community in general. Another option would be to have two panels documenting children's learning that would be appropriate for multiple audiences, with the third panel to be customized for different audiences. For example, when displayed at the veterinary clinic that hosted the class, the third panel could be a thank-you from the students. When the display is moved to other community locations, the third panel could mention ways community members could get involved with the schools, including promotion of the school's "volunteer grandparent" program, an item that would be particularly relevant when the display was located at the community senior citizen's center. Sometimes a display will travel around a community for a year or more—that's a lot of strategic communication impact for the effort required to create a single display.

WEBSITES

With 70% of homes with children under 18 having Internet access, according to the Annenberg Public Policy Center's "Media in the Home" survey (Woodward & Gridina, 2000), the Internet cannot be ignored as a communication tool for schools and centers. Although the lack of Internet access by even one family in a school or center excludes dependence on it for primary communication, schools would be wise to understand that many of their families go to the computer first for information. Community members, business professionals, and the media will also be likely to look for information on a school's website. A school that claims to provide students with what they need to compete in a technological world but doesn't have an up-to-date website or a staff that uses e-mail for regular communication lacks credibility. Yet often teachers who spend time shopping, looking up movie schedules, e-mailing, and even taking graduate courses online seem to think it is perfectly acceptable that parents and the community be forced to use other forms of communication to find out more than basic information about the school. Of course, some schools are taking advantage of this medium with the following features on their websites:

- Up-to-date calendars of events
- Invitations to events open to the community
- Portfolios of children's work for parent viewing with access codes
- Individual classroom pages with news from the classroom (sometimes updated daily)
- Schoolwide performance on standardized or state-required achievement tests
- Homework assignments
- The stories of projects or units of studies
- School board minutes, personnel notices, and legal postings

However, our survey of school websites revealed that most of these features are not being utilized. What is most often observed on these websites, however, is basic information about schools, statements of philosophy, lists of staff, schoolwide performance on tests, and legal notices. Even award-winning websites consist of geographic, legal, enrollment, and contact information with some calendars. Information on individual schools or centers frequently consists of outdated pages or pages with "under construction" signs. Rarely found on center and school websites are the following:

- Evidence other than test scores of how schools are achieving standards
- Examples of outstanding student work for public viewing
- Examples of how other constituencies such as corporations, community volunteers, or parents are involved in the schools and evidence of the impact these have on student learning

Center or school websites that do include student work or evidence of student learning other than test scores rarely provide information on the relationship of that work to standards or explanations of how the work connects with curriculum goals. The majority of websites viewed had no information about curriculum goals at all!

In talking with principals and directors about their use of school and center websites, we often hear that there is a lack of personnel to update and maintain the website. In the days when website design required designers to use HTML and difficult upload file transfers, website maintenance required extensive technology skills. Today the scanners and digital cameras with processing software and websites with built-in templates have made it very easy for anyone to update a website with no programming knowledge at all. It is possible for a district to have a website with links to school websites that a school secretary can access and update and for a school or center to have links to smaller websites for classrooms that can be accessed and updated by the teacher. This enables those on the front lines whose job responsibility includes communicating to take control of this media channel and not be dependent on technology staff to update and maintain the site. Community organizations often lag behind schools in technology use.

Another concern expressed by administrators is that something inappropriate might be posted to the website if the posting did not go through one person. We have found that requiring one person to review and approve everything that appears on a website has become a bottleneck inhibiting the timely use of this media channel. Schools and centers may want to re-examine this policy. If paper-format class notes or newsletters need not be approved before they are sent home, then should this be required for posting on the Internet website? If approval by an immediate supervisor is all that is required of paper versions, then this should be adequate for posting on a website. School districts should reexamine their policy on the use of their website to be sure that it encourages instead of discourages usage of this medium. One solution is to include rules for the use of this medium in training of primary credible communicators and to meet with staff and set guidelines for posting. Formatting can distinguish between individual web pages and school-controlled material.

With today's technology, websites can be convenient, inexpensive places to display documentation of student learning. Project or unit-of-study narratives are one convenient way to incorporate documentation into a website. PowerPoint or similar presentation software can be used to tell the story of an investigation of a topic by a class and placed on the website.

Even children as young as preschoolers can dictate narratives to go with photos and work samples. Children as young as 2nd graders often design their own PowerPoint or other media productions, revealing not only their writing skills but also the vocabulary they mastered during the project, the depth of their understanding, and their enthusiasm for the topic. Older students can take complete responsibility for the production. Teachers can add information such as state standards or curriculum goals. Sometimes these productions are developed while the investigation is ongoing and serve as journals, with daily or weekly updates. Families and other staff members follow the progress of the investigation as it evolves. This becomes a little like watching a soap opera and can engage everyone in the children's learning experience. The University Primary School has several projects that remain online for viewing. These can be viewed along with "Who Measures What in Our Neighborhood" (see Figure 6.3) at *www.ed.uiuc.edu/ups*. Teachers will often print pages for those children who do not have access to the Internet and send these home.

These online project narratives have also enabled community members or experts who have been consulted during the investigation to see the outcome of the project and evidence of what the children have learned from the experience. They will sometimes e-mail encouragement or suggestions for additional inquiries.

Another way to integrate documentation into websites is to illustrate how students achieve learning objectives or standards. Many public schools post (in fact, they may be required to post) results of student achievement tests. The school website provides an opportunity to provide additional evidence of student learning besides test scores. For example, why not link pages where test results are posted to documentation of how math concepts are taught and work examples. In Strategy Three, "Convince with Evidence," we learned how documentation can be convincing, powerful, and memorable. One of the advantages of the technology of a website is that it gives viewers control over the delivery of information. In written communication media such as newsletters or brochures, the writer must constantly be concerned about providing too much information and discouraging the reader. With the web, viewers determine how much information they want and how deeply they want to explore the topic.

One caution on the use of the Internet involves the posting of children's photos and names. Photos can be selected that focus on children's work and that show children in groups or in other situations where they are not easily identifiable. Posting of children's names, work, and/or photos on openly accessible sites on the Internet always requires the permission of parents. Generally when this is done, no names are used. Class news and information containing children's names and photos is often made available to parents on a site where access is controlled.

BROCHURES

Informational brochures or schedules of activities are another communication channel used by educational institutions. Childcare centers and preschools usually have a brochure that outlines their services and fees. School districts have brochures that describe services and explain how to enroll and access services. Private schools and educational programs provided by museums and other community organizations are dependent on the effectiveness of these brochures for enrollment and participation in their programs. More information on deciding what to put in brochures is available in Chapter 11, Foundation Builders.

Documentation can enhance the success of brochures by providing evidence of learning that occurs when participants use the services. Let us examine the brochures produced by the education staff of the

Chicago Children's Museum. In their brochure they had typically provided information about the field trip experiences available for area schools. In addition to hosting the class visits, the museum provides activities for teachers to do before the children come to the exhibit and when they return to their classrooms. Trained museum educators work with the teacher and children during the visit to maximize the quality of the learning experience.

The museum educators believe that the result for the children is more than a bus trip and a good time away from the classroom. They decided that they wanted to communicate more effectively in the brochure to enable readers to see this extended value of field trips. They selected a group of teachers whose classes were scheduled to visit the museum and introduced the concept of documentation and the collection of evidence. The teachers then shared the documentation with museum staff and discussed what was most meaningful to them about the experience. This documentation was then incorporated into the next brochure of field trip options sent out by the museum. Color Plate 4 shows a portion of the brochure and how the documentation was used.

ORGANIZING COMMUNICATION EVENTS

Many events are held by schools, libraries, childcare centers, and other educational agencies that are designed for the specific purpose of communicating about what is happening in their programs. These include open houses, science fairs, project nights, parent nights, visitation days, and parent conference days. These are excellent opportunities to share documentation for strategic communication.

These events, although intended to show how education is occurring, often do not focus on what is being learned. These events can be more effective if they are planned as strategic communication events. The event should focus on what and how students learned and the achievements from the learning experience. Opportunities to view evidence of learning should be a major part of the event, not peripheral to it.

For example, many open houses are held at schools to acquaint parents with the teacher and show what their child will be learning in school. At some schools these consist of parents dropping in, seeing where their child sits, seeing some artwork, and having punch and cookies in the gym. Open houses can be strategically designed to focus more on learning. In schools where children's work is documented, displays of typical changes in skills show parents what they can expect of their child this year. A brief explanation is given of the assessment system and how communication will occur between home and family, and copies of the learning goals are distributed. The first entries in their child's portfolio are available for them to examine. A story of a project or investigation, including how parents were involved, from the previous year is included. Parents build enthusiasm for the upcoming year and get the clear message that this is a school where learning occurs.

In addition to annual fall open houses, special events can be planned specifically for the purpose of sharing documentation, such as portfolio nights, when children's work is displayed and celebrated; project nights, when each class displays documentation of a topic they investigated; or science learning nights, when science investigations are on display. Any topic can be used for an open house in which children's work is spotlighted and displayed. Many schools have learned to use PowerPoint or other media software, sometimes including video sequences, for documentation. This enables them to create a media event based on student learning. Older students can take primary responsibility in the production. The showing becomes an event that children, parents, family members, and the community can attend. Additional displays of documentation can supplement the media.

NEWSLETTERS

Newsletters are a standard communication technique of most education-focused institutions. The purpose of most school or center newsletters is to update parents or other participants and provide relevant information about what has happened or what is about to happen in the program. Some schools have classroom newsletters, some have center or school newsletters, some have district newsletters, and some have a combination of these or even all of these. Some are daily, some weekly, some monthly, and some unscheduled. Some newsletters are professionally designed, some are handwritten, and some are student-generated.

Newsletters can be effective components of a communications plan if the educators think strategically about their design and use. Yet we rarely see newsletters that include documentation of student learning. We typically see lots of photos of events or stories about what children did, but few attempts are made to share what was learned or evidence of that learning. There are numerous ways that student work can be effectively integrated into newsletters—from banners to articles to photos.

Banners

The banner is the first thing a reader sees at the beginning of the communication process. The banner is the headline that spans the width of the opening page with the name of the organization, subtitles (called taglines), and other basic information about your newsletter. A tagline on a banner is "prime real estate" for focusing your message and should not be wasted on cute names or simple labeling. Strategic design of the banner should tell readers the type of information contained, to whom the newsletter is addressed, and the purpose of the newsletter.

For example, the tagline of a newsletter addressed to parents or primary caregivers could emphasize partnership, teaming, or working together and how this benefits their children's learning. The tagline of a newsletter addressed to members of the community might emphasize how student learning will benefit the community and communicate that the center is a learning environment. The examples in Figure 8.1 show how thinking strategically can improve the effectiveness of template-designed banners.

Student work can also be permanently incorporated into a banner. For example, the bee paintings in Figure 6.2 in Chapter 6 were incorporated into the banner design for the Discovery Preschool newsletter in Figure 8.1. Those new to the preschool may be curious about the heading. If the documentation is on display in the center, readers will recognize the work and be motivated to view the display. Those already familiar with the documentation will be reminded of the story each time they see the newsletter. At the very least, the banner for the newsletter, which becomes a "logo" or graphic representing the center, is focused on children's achievements rather than on the commercially made clip-art used in the banner of the Tiger Tots newsletter.

Sometimes parents and community audiences find a particular piece of documentation to be particularly powerful and meaningful. When this happens, those pieces of documentation can become part of the historical identity of the program and used not only in the banner but also on stationery, hangings, signs, business cards for staff—or even placemats for family restaurants.

Articles

Another way to integrate documentation into newsletters is to make documentation of student learning the focus of columns or articles. A regular column

Figure 8.1. Banner without strategic design (top) and with strategic design (bottom). The top banner is cute and eye catching but wastes an opportunity to communicate. The bottom banner strategically emphasizes learning, the history of the center (in the bee story), and provides necessary information.

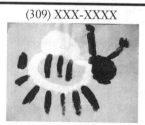

can be placed in the same location in each issue of the newsletter. This is an excellent way to use the message calendar that was discussed under Strategy Four, "Plan Your Message." For example, a column about how standards are achieved in a classroom can be addressed regularly in the lower right corner of the first page of a monthly newsletter, with each issue spotlighting a different area of the curriculum. During the course of the school year, work from all curriculum areas would be communicated. Another column could be reserved to share what children are learning in projects or integrated units. In each case these special columns featuring children's work will be most interesting if they include actual products, photos of children working, and/or pull quotes. *Pull quotes* are small sections of text that are pulled out, repeated in a margin or heading, and often enlarged for emphasis. Pull quotes of student writing or language are especially appealing.

Photos

Including photos of children working and samples of products from the learning experience captures the attention of the reader. The photos should add information to the article about the learning event, and the caption should include even more information about what children are learning. Figure 8.2 shows a life-size model of a boiler built by a prekindergarten classroom as well as a photo of the real boiler. The caption explicitly explains the relationship between the two photos. Without the photo of the real boiler, the significance of the parts that the children included in their model would be lost.

Including student work in a newsletter shows that learning is taking place every day in the school and that there is evidence of that. Parents and other readers don't have to wait for test score results to see if children are learning.

Get Strategic

Newsletters are more effective when they are meaningful for the receiver. Often educational programs try to have one newsletter to meet the needs of all constituencies with the idea that this saves time. However, a newsletter that risks not being relevant risks not being read. A newsletter ignored is a waste of time and money for everyone.

Thinking strategically about your newsletters would include asking yourself these questions:

- Who is the audience for this newsletter?
- How often will they see it?
- What messages would we like to communicate?
- Is there a message calendar to be followed (discussed in Strategy Four, "Plan Your Message")
- What types of learning will interest the recipients of this newsletter?

Figure 8.2. Children's boiler (top), real boiler (bottom). The boiler created by the preschoolers at Stone School in Brenda Dexter's classroom is impressive. However, the accuracy of their representation and their understanding of how it works is not evident until a photo of the real boiler is displayed next to it.

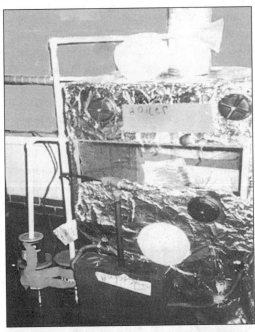

A strategic approach to communication would include different newsletters for different audiences. For example, an elementary school may have weekly Classroom Notes that teachers send out with specific information about what children are learning in their classrooms, logistical information about what children need to bring to school, dates to remember, and recognition of helpers. There may be a Parent Organization newsletter focusing on parent events and parent volunteer opportunities. The principal may have a monthly school newsletter for the whole school that highlights outstanding learning experiences, introduces school staff, and includes a calendar. There may be a newsletter for partners and corporate sponsors.

Although it takes more time to prepare different forms of communication or different versions of newsletters, these pay off in the success of the communication. With the availability of desktop publishing software, it is fairly easy to make templates for each newsletter, then copy and paste versions of those articles that would be meaningful from one to the other. If the corporate version of the newsletter goes out less frequently, it will likely be easy to fill it with only the relevant articles from the frequent parent newsletters.

We know from professional communicators that there are certain things that all readers prefer in newsletter design. These include carefully planned messages with a tight focus, short articles, attractive graphics, bulleted lists, and a clear organization system. They do not like newsletters that lack focus, have too much text, ramble, have too many pages, and/or offer irrelevant information. Other problems with newsletters include focusing on events that have already taken place rather than announcing or encouraging readers to attend upcoming events, not having the newsletter in the home languages of the audience, and not having an up-to-date calendar of all events. For many people, the calendar portion of a newsletter is the most useful. It is often saved and even posted on a refrigerator. Offering a relevant, useful calendar can be a way to ensure your newsletter gets read.

Once educators have made a newsletter strategic and professional-looking, the value of newsletters can be extended. Extra copies can be made available in a notebook for public viewing in the school office. These can be publicly displayed so that they can be consulted without asking staff for access. A current issue can be available on a bulletin board with a notebook of previous issues for consultation nearby. A phone number can be designated to call for a replacement newsletter when a copy has been lost. When staff refer to the newsletter, they also communicate its value. Extra copies of the newsletter can also be assembled into newsletter files that can be given to entering families to bring them up to date on what has happened at the school or center. Since most schools make electronic files of the print newsletters, these can easily be converted to PDF files so that they can be viewed on a website.

LESS FORMAL CLASSROOM COMMUNICATION PIECES

However, communications don't always need to be in the form of a newsletter. For example, a classroom teacher may find that producing a weekly or monthly newsletter requires too much time and prefers more frequent, less formal communication with families.

Figure 8.3. Field trip form. The non-strategically designed form on the left provides background information and is eye catching. However, the strategically designed form on the right achieves additional communication goals by using examples of children's work, by showing words the children are learning, and by giving explicit action goals.

We are going to the bakery!

The children became interested in baked goods after our bake sale and began to play bake sale. We are going to extend their learning by going to the bakery next Monday.

Please sign the permission form below.

- -

We are learning about bakeries!

When our parent group had the bake sale, our children began to play "bake sale" in our room. They made this sign for their play.

Words the children are learning:
bake sale   price   bakery
cookies   brownies   money
muffins   purchase

Illinois Early Learning standard: Print has meaning

To extend our children's learning, we are going to visit the bakery down the street next Monday. Please sign the permission form below.

- -

Weekly Class Notes may be effective as a handwritten then photocopied note as long as it still looks professional and the handwriting is easy to read. This kind of communication can highlight achievements of the last week, include topics for discussion within the family, and provide reminders for the upcoming week.

A teacher may prefer to use the informal Class Notes periodically in combination with a more formal newsletter. The Class Notes can refer to that more formal newsletter with the up-to-date calendar and the carefully created messages. One way to make the informal, more frequent news communication less time consuming is to make a template for this and make paper copies available for teachers to use as a master. There can be space for photos and children's work on Class Notes also. These can be reduced on a photocopy machine.

There are other communication opportunities with families that can be enhanced with documentation. There are some communication pieces that require every parent to read and respond. These are "prime real estate" for schools to convey how much students are learning. Two examples are requests for permission for field trips and requests for parents to sign up for parent–teacher conferences.

Figure 8.3 shows portions of two field trip permission forms for a visit to a bakery sent home by a preschool teacher at the beginning of a project on bakeries. The form on the left is attractive, uses appropriate clip-art, and looks professional. However, the revised field trip request on the right strategically communicates that this is a learning experience. The clip-art has been replaced with authentic work of the children. The paragraph explains the significance of the work. By including the Illinois Early Learning

Standard, the teacher adds credibility to the learning experience.

Figure 8.4 shows a communication informing parents about parent–teacher conferences and requesting that they sign up for a time. The original version on the left looks friendly and professional, communicates the purpose of the conference, and asks for participation. However, this is a missed opportunity to do much more. In the revised version on the right, a photograph of parents at a previous conference replaces clip-art. A different photo can be used for each notice. Over 1 or 2 years, parents will see a variety of family configurations in conferences (sometimes two parents, sometimes a grandmother, sometimes a single parent) and a variety of racial and ethnic cultures participating. The revised version specifically states what the parent will see and do and what they should do or bring to the conference (action goal). It also indicates a focus for this conference that tells the parents why this conference is different from other conferences. It is likely that the school is using a message calendar focusing on different areas of learning throughout the year.

These are just two "prime real estate" opportunities for communication with parents. Schools and centers would find it advantageous to take the time to reflect on those events during the year requiring communication that every parent must read and respond to.

In this chapter, we have shared many ways that documentation can be incorporated into communication opportunities for education institutions. In the next chapter we will share design conventions from professional communicators so you can make your communications look professional and credible.

Figure 8.4. Parent conference form. The non-strategically designed form on the left gets the job done. However, the strategically designed form on the right is more inclusive, provides action goals, recognizes parents who attended last time, and gives information to make it easier for parents who haven't come before.

It is time for parent conferences!

We are looking forward to hearing from you how you think things are going. We will also share with you your child's portfolio and our assessment process. Please sign up for a 20-minute time slot below so we can meet together. It is important that you come and show your support for your child.

Please indicate the best time for your conference below.

- - - - - - - - -

Mr. and Mrs. Whitney look at Clarissa's portfolio at the last conference.

Habits of mind we monitor: Predicting, asking questions, hypothesizing, being curious

It is time for parent conferences!

We are looking forward to hearing from you how *you think* things are going. We will also share with you your child's

- portfolio (emphasizing habits of mind this time)
- work samples
- observation log
- documentational milestones checklist

Bring any questions you have or work your child has done at home.

Please indicate the best time for your conference below.

- - - - - - - - -

CHAPTER 9

Strategy 6

Follow Design Conventions: Making Communication Look Professional

Although you may not be able to learn everything that professional communicators know about design, you can learn some basic principles and incorporate them into your communication process. Following these design principles can improve the effectiveness of communication, enhance the credibility of the evidence, and foster the respect of a community for a school or center and the staff. Sharing children's work, like displaying artifacts in a museum, is both an art and a science.

KEEP YOUR FOCUS ON YOUR MESSAGE

Before any choices are made on type of media, font size, or photos, you will want to start by reflecting on what you want to say. When taking on a communication task such a preparing a display for a shopping mall, there is a natural tendency to jump directly to design decisions such as selecting what will be eye-catching or what colors you might use. However, the number one consideration of your communication is always the content of what you want to communicate, the nature of your audience, and what you are trying to accomplish.

When first learning how to use documentation as a communication strategy, teachers have found it helpful to think of opening one of these three windows:

- *Window on a learning experience*: Will telling the story of a learning experience interest this audience? Is there a learning experience I can share that will accomplish my strategic communication goals?
- *Window on a child's development*: Do I have documentation of an individual child's or student's growth that is especially powerful and that illustrates the point I want to make?
- *Window on teacher reflection*: Do I need to share my own thoughts or those of my colleagues to get my point across? Do others need to see the learning process or my classroom through my eyes? How might that help accomplish my communication goals?

Keeping communication goals or a message calendar (described in Strategy Four, "Plan Your Message") displayed where you are working on your documentation will remind you of your goals and keep you from being overwhelmed by the wealth of documentation and evidence that you have. Perhaps you can open a window on one of those goals. Remember that it isn't necessary to tell everything; rather, choose what will do the best job communicating what you want to communicate.

Always begin by reflecting on what you want to communicate and clarifying your focus. When you have a clear understanding of what you want to say, then you can start thinking about design and display issues.

DESIGN PRINCIPLES

We can learn about design principles from exhibit designers who have studied the science of display; from photographers and artists who communicate through images; and from graphic designers who produce professional newsletters, posters, advertisements, and displays. Many of the design principles apply to all of these. Some are specific for one type of communication. However, all of these principles apply to educator-communicators who want to communicate effectively. To simplify sharing these principles with others and teaching them in workshops, we have grouped them into three categories: photos, graphic design, and display.

Taking Good Photos

Photographs are powerful communication tools. A good photograph alone can often tell a story. In visiting schools and viewing documentation of student learning, we are often saddened that wonderful learning experiences are so poorly documented photographically and are therefore difficult to share with others. This is like sending a lawyer into a courtroom with no evidence. It is one thing to talk about how children tried several approaches to building a structure before they made one that could stand, but the effect is entirely different when the children are photographed at each step and then in triumph when they solved the problem.

Good photos don't happen by accident. However, we do not want educators to be distracted from the educational process by worrying extensively about the quality of photos for documentation. There are simple things that can be done to improve the quality of photos for documentation.

Digital Cameras. In our work with teachers in classrooms doing documentation, we have come to rely on digital cameras with automatic focus and zoom features. These are now available with good resolution, and educator-communicators should use a high-resolution setting so that the photos can be enlarged for strategic communication.

The biggest advantage of digital cameras is that they enable educators to take multiple shots in sequence without worrying about making each shot count, so they can still keep their focus on supporting learning. The best photos can be saved and the rest deleted. They can be viewed immediately and retaken to be sure important moments are not missed.

Digital photos are easy to crop and enlarge; it is also easy to correct their lighting and contrast. They can be quickly and easily inserted into newsletters, displays, websites, and electronic presentations. Digital photos allow immediate sharing with children, parents, and the media. In the long run, digital photos save money and time for schools and centers.

Picture-Taking Skills. Children should be photographed in action, not posing. Action shots draw observers into the learning experience. What is happening? What are they doing? Do not take photos of students standing up holding their work in front of them. Contrast the two photos in Figure 9.1. These photos were taken by a family home childcare provider, DeCarla Burton, to document a project on worms. They are both appealing photos. In the first photo, the child is aware of the photographer, and the viewer's attention quickly focuses away from the learning experience to looking at the background. However, the photo of children digging sparks much more curiosity on the part of the viewer. What are they digging for? Did they find anything?

You should photograph the result of the educational process—children's work. This is a convenient and inexpensive way of keeping an electronic copy of students' work on file along with photographic documentation. Action photographs that feature students in the process of producing their work combined with photos of samples of that work are especially powerful. A photo of a 3-year-old sketching a fire truck that he is studying displayed next to his drawing enables adults to see what the child is representing and the meaningfulness of the drawing. A 6th grader's drawing showing the result of a science experiment next to a photograph of him performing the experiment is much more interesting and revealing than the work alone.

Check the background of your shot before you click. This is the one rule it is important to consider before you push the button. If the background shows dirty snack dishes on the counter or a messy teacher's desk or a student with a questionable t-shirt slogan—any of which might keep you from sharing the photograph—then don't take it. By checking the background first, you can alter that background by pointing the camera downward and focusing more on the work. Or you could move your body around to another

Figure 9.1. Child with playground in background (top), children digging for worms (bottom). In the top photo, the background is distracting and the child looking into the camera does not show learning. The bottom photo focuses on what the children are doing and also reveals some of the skills and enthusiasm for the project.

One way to get great-looking photos is to use the rule of thirds. When using the rule of thirds, draw two imaginary parallel lines from top to bottom and from side to side in your viewfinder. "If you frame your pictures so that . . . your children are located where any two lines intersect, or along any of the lines, the picture will be more visually appealing . . . more natural and lifelike" (Morgan & Thaler, 1996, p. 27). Keeping children or children's work on the lines and especially near the intersections of the lines is an easy way to produce great-looking photos (see Figure 9.2). Using the rule of thirds explains the appeal of many good photos but especially of photos that effectively capture children's learning.

Of course, most teachers don't have the time or the inclination to think about such things during the educational process. They are too focused, as they should be, on helping children learn. There is, however, a solution—cropping! The secret to successful photos is often not how the photo looks at the moment it was taken but how it looks after parts of it are cut away or eliminated.

When I (Judy) was a yearbook editor, I learned a fast trick I still use—cropping L's (see Figure 9.3). These can be made out of heavy card stock in several different sizes and used repeatedly. They can also be made out of any paper at anytime for one-time use. On the yearbook staff we called this "mining for good

Figure 9.2. Photo of children drawing a picture of a combine with rule of thirds lines marked on the photo. Cropping a photo so the points of greatest eye appeal are around the intersection of the lines results in more interesting photos.

side so the background is different or the offending t-shirt or view is blocked. Another alternative is to use your zoom to focus tightly on the student and work, so there is no background visible at all.

It is a good idea to fill the picture with children or student work even if the background is pleasing. When composing a photograph, get close or zoom in. Unless there is a significant reason to show the background (e.g., to emphasize the size of the student compared with the size of a fire truck), fill the picture with what you want your audience to focus on—in education that would be student learning and student work. Think of your camera as a spotlight. Focus it on what you think is important and your audience will see it as important, too.

Figure 9.3. Photo with cropping L's. Two pieces of paper cut into L shapes can be moved around on the photo to try different ways of cropping.

Figure 9.4. First photo of Alex and spider, not cropped. Look at the photo and write a quick caption about what Alex is learning; then look at the second photo below.

Figure 9.5. Second photo of Alex and spider, cropped. What does this photo emphasize about this learning experience? What stands out the most in each photo?

photos." By placing the two L's on a photo to make the borders of a rectangle and moving them around, various ways of cropping the photo can be tested to find the most effective photo. Often parts of a photo are revealed that are not so easily seen when the whole photo is viewed. Cropping L's work just as well on a computer screen when using photo-editing software as they do on a printed photo. Before using the cropping tools provided by the software, you can place your L's directly on the photo as it appears on the screen and experiment with various ways you could crop the photo before you begin to use the software tools. The L's makes it easy and fast to see the many options before cropping digitally. Using cropping L's and applying the rule of thirds have yielded excellent documentation photos for busy educators.

By cropping you can focus the viewer on certain parts of an experience. In Figure 9.4 we see the first photo of Alex. Look at the photo and write a quick caption about what Alex is learning. Now look at Figure 9.5, a cropped version of the photo of Alex. They are different. What does this photo emphasize about this learning experience? What stands out the most in each photo? Most people see the spider in the photo in Figure 9.4, but in Figure 9.5, they notice Alex's interaction with the book or his emotional involvement in the experience. Cropping the photo so that Alex's expression can be seen and applying the rule of thirds so that the book, his eye, and the magnifying glass are on those magical lines means the viewer thinks more about Alex's learning to use books to look up things. This photo more effectively communicates about emotional involvement in learning and the value of books and literacy.

In general, audiences will respond more to seeing emotional involvement in learning experiences. In taking photos for documentation, capture the emotion of the moment. In Figure 9.6 the two preschoolers are discovering green moss on one of their first spring walks. Even though their faces are not seen

Figure 9.6. Preschoolers looking at moss. This photo of pre-schoolers on a spring walk captures their emotions when they discover a patch of green moss. Photos showing emotional involvement such as this one draw in viewers.

Figure 9.7. Writing corn words. This photo, shot from above, captures not only the children working but also the product of their work. They are writing the title "Corn Food" for a display of food products that contained corn which they had collected.

clearly, their body positions indicate fascination and shared curiosity.

One way to show children's work and children in action at the same time is to shoot from above. This works especially well for writing, art activities, science experiences, or any learning activities that involve the use of children's hands. In Figure 9.7 children are making a title "Corn Food" for a display of food products that contained corn they had collected. Shooting down enables both the children and the work to be captured. Showing children creating work along with the work increases the credibility of the work because it makes the viewer feel more like an eyewitness.

Outside action shots are another simple way to add interest and show that learning does not occur only in a schoolroom. Outdoor photos are often more colorful and more interesting because of the good lighting and the variation in background and texture. The photo of children sketching the parts of a combine shown in Figure 9.2 as an example of the rule of thirds is pleasant and memorable because it shows children working outside.

Although digital photos are easy to work with and easy to store, the biggest mistake that nonprofessionals make in working with digital photos is in altering proportions. This happens when the photo is lengthened or widened. The result is a photo that looks stretched or squashed. The excellent photo from Smart Start Early Childhood Center shown in Figure 9.8 would lose its effectiveness if it were stretched too tall or squashed too short, as also shown in the figure. This gives photos an amateurish look. Generally this can be avoided in any photo-processing program by decreasing or increasing the size of a photo only by pulling on the corners, not the sides of the photo. Check your program manual for directions. If you must change the shape of a photo to fit a space, cropping is a better solution than changing proportions. The ideal approach is to crop your photo as appropriate for your message and the photo aesthetics, and then work your layout around the dominant photos, rather than fitting the photo into a space—if it doesn't fit, the space may need adjusting, not the photo!

Using Graphic Elements Effectively

One window that professional communicators can open for educators is a window into good design principles. These design principles can be applied to all school communications—from websites to notes home, from newsletters to displays at the mall. To communicate effectively requires an understanding of the use of the graphic elements of text, photos, drawings, display items, and white space. Too often good-quality photographs and meaningful documentation are not as effective as they could be. We saw an excel-

Figure 9.8. Three photos—the original (top photo) and two examples of improper photo manipulation (middle and bottom photos). When inserting digital photos into newsletters and displays, the most common mistake made is the altering of proportions. This happens when the photo is lengthened (middle photo) or widened (bottom photo) instead of enlarging or reducing by pulling on the corners of the digital image. Stretching (middle photo) or squashing (bottom photo) photos should be avoided.

lent collection of children's work that was thoughtfully selected and carefully planned to show how children meet Illinois early learning goals through active, engaged learning experiences. However, it lost effectiveness because it was mounted on colored construction paper, was arranged poorly on the materials, had many small photos, and lacked an overall design plan. This gave the display an overall amateur or bulletin board impression.

No one expects educators to spend time and effort in becoming a graphic designer before they do a class newsletter or to become a museum curator before they do a display. Fortunately, there are a number of resources that make these design principles accessible. Easy-to-use desktop publishing software providing templates with built-in design principles enable a plug-and-publish approach that results in professional-looking publications. These can be adapted to include documentation—directions and several examples are provided in Chapter 12, Tools for Opening Windows. In addition, templates are available for download on our website *http://www.bestpracticesinc.net*.

Several books provide condensed and simplified design principles for use by nondesigners. Our favorite is Robin Williams's *Non-Designer's Design Book* (2003), which is humorous, well-illustrated, and easy to follow. Williams selects the following principles as most important for the nondesigner to understand:

- *Contrast:* There should be a contrast among the print, fonts, photos, and text, as well as light and dark elements, on a page or on a display.
- *Alignment:* Elements should line up. Check displays and pages for "invisible lines." For example, photo edges should line up with caption text.
- *Proximity:* Those things that have shared meaning should be grouped together. Captions should be next to photos.
- *Repetition:* Use the same elements such as a font or a figure or a color throughout to give the display or document a professional look.

Other design elements that are helpful to know about include visual weight; directionality; and white, or negative, space. All items have a sense of weight. Darker photos and text look heavier. Generally heavy items look better at the bottom of a display or page. Another element, directionality, also impacts time spent looking at or studying a page or display. Some items have strong directionality. We pick up cues to the directionality from the faces of individuals, what the individuals in the photos would be seeing, lines such as power lines, and even lines such as the edges of books in the photo. We are more comfortable and will look longer when we are directed back toward the center of the display, not off the edge.

Eye-catchers such as colorful borders or commercial art that are not focused on students or student work distract attention from your messages. Student work and what they are learning should take center stage. Borders, text frames, and photos all can take focus away from what children are learning.

Other basic design advice is to avoid the use of monotonous rows of photos or objects that are all the same. These are boring. The viewer rarely has the time or inclination to look at all of them and therefore reasons that coming back later is the best option. Later never happens! The concept in Strategy Four, "Plan Your Message," that less is more also applies to graphic design.

Displaying Student Work

The display of student work can be enormously powerful when well done. Since displays are large and people must actively choose what to look at, moving their eyes and even their bodies to see different sections, their design poses special problems. The basic design principles of contrast, repetition, alignment, and proximity apply to display, but other issues also must be considered. Displays are often viewed by people standing or on the move and usually by people who are totally controlling their own time. Much can be learned from museum exhibit designers about display.

Again we see the idea that less is more. This is especially true of the amount of text that can be used in displays. "Good exhibitions are conceptually simple. The more complex the verbal message becomes, the less understandable the exhibition turns out to be, since exhibitions are basically nonverbal enterprises" (Gurian, 1996, p. 4). Even though the concept of "holding power" (Miles & Tout, 1990)—the amount of time spent by a viewer looking at a particular exhibit—is an important consideration, display designers should take heart that much is absorbed by casual viewing. Viewers can be reading a display even when it looks as though they are not. The average literate person processes print at 250 to 300 words per minute and will read about 20 words or more in the 5 seconds he or she walks toward or by an exhibit (McManus, 1990). The point is to make those words count. One of the ways to do that is to take advantage

of what museum display designers refer to as a conversational relationship with the viewer. In museums it is the idea that a museum "someone" is talking to them. In educational displays that someone is probably an educator-communicator.

Imperative and interrogative statements are often used effectively in display headings (McManus, 1990): "Look for the differences between these two writing samples." "What do you think the children learned about gravity?" Sometimes it is helpful to use a heading to anticipate and point out what might be confusing. Research is showing that viewers bring an active sense-making process to displays, and it is important to anticipate what might be confusing or misunderstood (Rowan, 1990). Such headings as "This might not look like writing to you" could avoid confusion for a reader who did not know that early writing includes letter-like shapes, not real letters. Even better, the heading "Is this really writing?" not only confronts a possible area of confusion but uses a question to draw the viewer into the display. Of course, the display should enable the viewer to answer or find the answer to the question.

Keeping the focus on children's work and your message is fairly easy with today's technology. Use labels in displays that approximate the color of the background. The easiest is to use white labels on white display boards or display areas; however, many museums print text on clear labels that can then be placed on color backgrounds. This works if the background is subtle and does not itself distract from the work of the children. It is also possible to print text on clingy plastic static stickers that can be used inside display cases or windows. All of these are available for standard color inkjet printers.

Display Techniques. The series of photos in Color Plate 5 illustrate some standard display techniques and the effect they have on viewers' ability to focus on the learning occurring. In example a and example b, the star shape and quote balloon, which were designed to attract attention to the display, capture the eye but draw attention *away* from the children working together and what they are learning. The strong border in example c, while attractive, also detracts from the focus on learning. The border on the text in example d makes the text box appear heavy and unbalanced. Although adding a border to the photo in example e balances the composition, it also creates a white space in the center that draws attention to itself. Generally the best and most professional looking display is to have text appear as a supplement to the photo or work sample. In example f, by placing the text close to the photo without a border and enlarging the photo, the focus of the viewer is on the children working and learning together and on the words they are writing.

In Color Plate 6, a display is altered to illustrate how the use of graphic design principles can impact effectiveness. The series begins with a typical bulletin board approach to putting up photos of a field trip. At each revision, design principles are applied to transform it into a more meaningful and focused communication panel.

Hanging Work. When hanging displays, remember that the human eye is lazy and usually looks only ahead and down. Share children's work with them in the classroom at their height, but do not expect adults to stoop to view it at a lower level if you want them to really read it. Hang work for adults with the center at about 5 feet 3 inches. The comfortable viewing area for adults is a band of about 4 feet—2 feet above and 2 feet below eye level.

When work is hung, horizontal and vertical center alignment are more pleasing. Flush alignment, with all the top edges lined up, looks unnatural and contrived in hanging displays. Many schools have installed tack strips, which make putting up student work quick and easy; however, it encourages flush alignment, which discourages viewing. Tacking work in the middle or hanging a paper backdrop from the tack strip can enable a more natural alignment.

Display things in their natural way. If the children make a butterfly, hang it in the air. Collected items from outdoors can be displayed on burlap. Displaying student work with the real items that inspired them also creates more interest—especially if the items themselves are of interest.

A FINAL NOTE ON DESIGN PRINCIPLES

Remember to keep the audience in mind. A focused display is more effective, and a display with a few selected elements is often more likely to be viewed, read, and remembered!

CHAPTER 10

Strategy 7

Reach Out to the Media: Connecting with Your Community

Media (plural of noun *medium*) 1) The main means of mass communication, especially newspapers, radio and television; the reporters, journalists, etc., working for organizations engaged in such communication.

Medium: 3a) An intervening substance through which a force acts on objects at a distance or through which impressions are conveyed to the senses. 3b) A pervading or enveloping substance; the substance in which an organism lives or is cultured. . . . 5) An intermediate agency, instrument or channel; a means; specifically, a channel of mass communication (The Shorter Oxford English Dictionary, 2002)

THE MASS NEWS MEDIA—newspapers, magazines, radio, and television—are a key audience for educator-communicators. The main reason is that they are channels by which the real key audience can be reached—the general audience of people in our society. Thus, the mass media are an important audience mainly because they are a means to reach a larger audience. In fact, the mass media are effectively the only efficient way to reach the masses. Direct mail is not cost-efficient for many educational institutions, and community events and direct interaction reach very few people at a time. When you have a message to deliver to the masses, the mass media are the best channel of communication.

The word *media* has become synonymous with the mass media, but a look at the original definitions of the term *medium* gives us some insight into the roles the mass media play in society. As quoted above, the mass media can be thought of as "an instrument or chan-nel," "an intervening substance" through which news sources can reach their audiences. But the news media are not just a "substance," but people with their own minds; they are gatekeepers who control access to the wider audience. The most efficient way to get a message to the wider community is to convince those in the mass media of the importance of the message and let them deliver the message for you.

Another reason the mass news media are a key audience for educators is that newspapers, magazines, radio, and television make up that "pervading or enveloping substance" in which members of our society live and are acculturated. They are the primary public forum, a window through which we look at our world. The mere presence of issues and people in the news media defines them as important. Children's learning should be seen as an important issue, which means it needs to have a presence in the mass media.

News media do see education as an important issue, and they do devote news time and space to it, although those who are directly involved in educating children may not always be happy with that coverage. Reporters do dig for information and try to find their own story ideas, and they do play the watchdog role in monitoring ongoing public institutions. Most news, however, is actually brought to them by people who want to reach that wide public audience. A great deal of news coverage of education issues does not come from educators, who are busy teaching and working with children, but from politicians. As representatives of the people, politicians are very interested at the societal level in the education of our children. More cynically, one might argue that politicians know that the people are very concerned about education, and so they are highly motivated to demonstrate to their voters that they are doing something about it, and they also have professional public relations staff dedicated to publicizing their views and actions on such issues. Given the limited or even nonexistent public relations staff at many schools, centers, and other educational organizations, reaching out to the news media often does not make the priority list. If educators do not bring their news to the attention of the news media, it is not surprising that news media coverage of education does not emphasize the educators' perspective.

Think back to the example at the opening of this book, in which the 2nd-grade teacher reads the scathing letter to the editor calling for a back-to-basics, drill-and-practice approach. The writer of that letter is probably one of the many individuals whose main window on the educational process is the mass media. In our example, the teacher wishes she could somehow bring that writer to her classroom. If that individual is a parent or happens to become involved as a guest speaker or a field trip host, there would be opportunities for the teacher to open that window for him on the real education process going on in the classroom. But it is quite likely that the mass media will continue to be the main window on education for this concerned citizen. One solution is to make sure that the window he does have offers a view with insight and meaning, and the way to do that is to reach out to the news media. Open a window for the news media, and you open it for the wider audience they serve. This chapter discusses ways to reach out to small-scale news media that might be interested in local "soft news" from educators in their community. Working with them at the local level is easier than many people think.

A WIN–WIN SITUATION

Local reporters typically have a strong community spirit and are very aware of their role in providing information readers, viewers, or listeners will use to improve their communities. Like teachers, they know that audiences are not always as motivated as they should be to learn the information they need to know. They want to find entertaining ways to bring large issues, such as education, to their audiences' attention.

Local news media must compete with myriad national and special-interest media. Short on staff, time,

resources, and clout, they can't compete on excitement, depth of news analysis, exclusive celebrity news, or slick publication. The one special thing they have to offer is the local, geographically specific nature of the news they cover. Thus, they need to cover local news well and make sure their audiences know it. Schools, childcare centers, park district programs, and other institutions where children learn are very local, and education of their children is one of the most important activities communities do together. This means local news media are likely to be interested in the learning of local children in general, and especially interested in the public institutions charged with this mission.

Amidst all those lofty principles, local reporters have very pressing practical concerns. On a weekly, daily, or even twice daily basis, they must fill a newspaper or broadcast. At a small newspaper, reporters may be expected to produce two or three stories per day; at a big-city newspaper, they may have several days to write a single story. At a small publication, with fewer staff, they also may be more dependent on community members for story ideas and information. At the national level, the challenge in filling that newspaper or broadcast is choosing among the myriad crises while still carving out some space for ongoing issues. Getting attention from the national media is difficult even for skilled professional communicators. At the local level, the challenge for reporters is often more about finding something going on and making it sound interesting and exciting—and getting that story or photo done in the short time frame available. Many local media would love to hear more from local educators because they need to fill a news hole. Big-city media are much like national media, and local educators may not have much luck getting coverage unless there is a really significant, urgent story. But even big cities likely have some news media outlets that have a more local focus, such as a weekly newspaper for a specific suburb. These smaller newspapers would make an excellent target for educators who want to reach out to a wider audience. Large newspapers may also have neighborhood or education-related sections that might make a good target.

For example, the small-town daily newspaper where I (Amanda) was a reporter needed a local photograph every day. (Because being perceived as *local* was so important, the newspaper policy was always to have a local photo on the front page.) While there was always news to report, much of this news did not make for an engaging, fresh photograph. Photos could often be more feature-like (less hard news) and stand alone without necessarily involving a whole story. At more than a few news meetings, our staff would be racking our brains for something that would make a decent photo, an action shot that could be viewed as somehow newsworthy. Our photographer, Christine Fortney, would start working through her list, calling different community organizations and institutions looking for one that had anything photographable. As part of her regular job as a news photographer, Ms. Fortney cultivated relationships with a number of potential sources for photos on a slow news day. Schools were on her list, and she had some luck with finding some photo opportunities. As more teachers and principals in the community saw the positive coverage others were getting, they started to contact her. Sometimes they would send a formal news release in advance; at other times they would call or send a fax the day of an event and simply say, "If you have time to drop in, this might make a good photo." The schools and teachers also learned to be cooperative. They learned what kinds of activities made good photos and where to find the blanket permission parents had signed.

"I'd much prefer taking pictures of kids *doing things*," Ms. Fortney said. "It took forever to get that through to people, but eventually I did get teachers to call me up so I could take a picture of an activity."

Initially, teachers she worked with wanted group photos of the whole class or all the students involved with a project, or they objected when a good action photo of a less motivated student was selected over a less interesting photo of a student who "deserved" to be featured in the newspaper. Eventually the educators she worked with learned to trust her professional judgment for what made a newsworthy, attention-getting photo.

"It was good for the school, good for the kids," Ms. Fortney said. "It was good for me to be able to go into the schools and see what they were actually doing, how they were learning. I was surprised at how much the community was involved in the education of the kids, sponsoring programs and working with the kids."

As the cooperative relationship developed, the local schools proved to be a good source for photos on slow news days, which over time meant the schools of Kirksville, Missouri, got a lot of positive coverage. In 1999, nominated by local teachers, the *Kirksville Daily Express* received an award from the Northeast District Teachers Association for its coverage of education in northeast Missouri.

This relationship was a win for all parties involved. It was good for the newspaper because it provided an engaging photo in a pinch and helped the newspaper toward its overall mission of being a window on the community. Furthermore, children are photogenic and naturally appealing to audiences, so the photos of children learning made attention-getting front-page material. It was also a source of positive community news. A major function of the news media is alerting people to problems, and problems that need to be solved tend to be seen as more critical than positive news that requires no action. This means news media tend to be full of negative news, which is important for readers to know but has a depressing overall effect. A positive photo helps balance this so that reading the newspaper is an enjoyable experience.

The relationship with the photographer was also good for the schools because their work was presented in a positive light. The ongoing work of the schools was brought to life for the community in snapshot views of children learning that symbolized what was going on in schools all the time. The photographer's surprise at the strong role of the community in children's education was probably shared by many of her readers, who needed that up-to-date window on what really happens in schools. It was also good for the children. Being featured in the newspaper, or seeing their classmates featured in the newspaper, gave them a voice in the public forum. It was a form of recognition from society that their activities are important and positively regarded. It was good for the community, the newspaper's audience, because the regular photos gave them an awareness of their local schools in an enjoyable way.

HOW CAN EDUCATORS REACH OUT TO LOCAL MEDIA?

The primary method of informing news media of an issue or event is a press release. This simply means writing up a story and submitting it to news media. You can also pass on to the media fliers or announcements about an event or give a reporter or photographer a call. However, the best way is to use a press release. Chapter 12, Tools for Opening Windows, provides a template showing the typical press release format.

Using the proper format sends a signal that you are a professional communicator, or at least that you communicate in a professional way. Receiving a properly formatted news release gives reporters and photographers confidence that you are a reliable source and that you have some understanding of working with the media. It signals to them that working with you will be pleasant because you understand their deadline pressure and the importance of accuracy. If you are planning to write a lot of press releases, it would be worth getting a copy of the *Associated Press Stylebook*. This journalists' "bible" covers all kinds of style and formatting issues. The format, however, is secondary to the information and the timing. The main issue is to include the necessary information and get the release out quickly. Figure 10.1 provides a checklist of information that should be included in a press release.

Press Release Content

A press release is usually written just like a news story. One reason for this is that the news staff may choose to use all or part of the press release as a news story. The more it sounds like a news story, the less editing they have to do. The less work they have to do, the more likely it will get used. The less editing they have to do, the more likely they are to print what you wanted them to print. It's not that the news staff are lazy; it's that they can't possibly do everything they have to do in the amount of time available—a situation that should sound familiar to educators!

Another reason press releases are written like news stories is that the inverted pyramid style of a news story (discussed in Strategy Four, "Plan Your Message") is just as helpful for a reporter or editor reading your

Figure 10.1. Press release checklist.

> ### Press Release Checklist
>
> ✓ Include all of the basic information about your story: who, what, when, where, why, and how. Make sure all this information is correct.
>
> ✓ Spell all names correctly and use official titles.
>
> ✓ Include the name, title, and telephone number of a person the reporter or photographer can contact with questions.
>
> ✓ Make sure the contact person can be reached by telephone during business hours. Consider providing additional contact names and numbers in case the primary one cannot be reached.
>
> ✓ Use facts to inform and quotes to persuade. Opinions and emotions make the story more interesting and get your point across, but they need to be in quotation marks.
>
> ✓ Include sources for statistics, research, and other supporting material.

Source: Adapted from Helm, A. (1999).

release as it is for audiences reading an article. The reporter or editor can get the critical information quickly. The first sentence will need to convince the reporter or editor that the article is worth printing or covering and the reader that it is worth reading. Crafting the writing is not so important—they will probably edit the writing anyway! Getting to the point quickly, having something worthwhile to say, and supporting it with good evidence are what's important.

Besides inverted pyramid style, the main thing that distinguishes news writing from other types of writing is that sources are clearly identified. Failure to identify sources and particularly to distinguish between facts and opinion is probably the most significant problem with press releases from "amateur" communicators. In news writing, the author, presumably a reporter, is relatively invisible in the story, theoretically a purely objective narrator. The sources of the facts are identified in attributions. Almost every piece of information in a news story will have an attribution tagged on to it, such as "according to principal Jane Smith," or "as stated in the Missouri State curriculum guide," or "said Joe Green, whose daughter is a member of Girl Scout Troop 29." The first reference to the source also mentions why that person is a credible source or why his or her statement is relevant. Unless the "facts" presented in the story are almost universally agreed on, a source is usually mentioned. It is not uncommon for almost every sentence to have an attribution. If a press release comes in without identifying sources, editors will not be able to run the information until sources are identified.

Furthermore, opinions and feelings *must* come from specific people—the news sources or members of the community the reporter covers—usually in the form of quotations. Reporters like to give the reader the sense that they are hearing news straight from the scene or straight from the people involved. Thus, they like to use a few quotations to liven up a story even when the source is not sharing a feeling or opinion. Opinions and feelings are quite interesting and are probably the most powerful way for educators to make their points. Reporters want to include them, but they must come from the news source, not the reporter or the news outlet.

When you are writing a press release, you are both the news source and, temporarily, the author. It is like writing a rough draft of the article to help the reporter get started. This means you must write as a reporter would write, attributing information to yourself and even quoting yourself in the press release. It may feel silly, but it doesn't sound silly when your quote shows up in a news article. By then, the reporter or the news media outlet is seen as the author. Sometimes a reporter will call for a real quote anyway, but the press release quote can serve as a back-up if you can't be reached. Providing a quote may help your release get into the news instead of languishing on the bottom of some reporter's long to-do pile.

As a newspaper reporter, I (Amanda) was frequently frustrated by the time spent trying to pin down specific individuals to quote after getting news releases from nonprofit organizations. For example, one news release included the statement, "What's so great about our new summer reading program is that it really involves parents, and children are much more likely to become lifelong readers if they see their parents in that role." The newspaper could not make that statement, yet the statement is critical to making the story seem important and making a point for readers. (Newspapers may have a bit of a vested interest in encouraging lifelong readers!) "What's so great . . ." is clearly a personal opinion. No newspaper would be able to repeat this claim except as a quotation. "Children are much more likely to become lifelong readers . . ." is more of a fact, but it needs to be attributed. If the news article states it as a fact, the reporter will have to try to track down some research source that says this. You can bet the reporter does not have time. A librarian, however, is an expert source. If the reporter had a specific local librarian to attribute it to, that problem could be easily resolved. A quote would be even better. Not only does the quote liven up the story for readers, but it makes it look like the reporter actually interviewed a local librarian without the reporter having to take the time to do it.

Better yet, the news release could attribute information to several sources, perhaps the library director, a librarian, and a parent and child participating in the program. Then the reporter's work is done, and the story is more likely to get into the paper. As discussed in Strategy Two, "Invest in the Most Credible Communicators," teachers, principals, and others who work with children are experts in their field and eyewitnesses to the learning in their classrooms. They make excellent sources for quotations that reflect excitement, ask for help, or share a professional opinion. Providing these quotations in the news release saves reporters a lot of time.

If you include quotations from other sources, the best way is to actually interview the other sources yourself. For example, a teacher might simply tell a parent she would like to include a parent comment in a press release and ask if the parent has something to say about

that particular project or issue. Another approach is to use comments you know the source said for another reason, such as quotations from children that were recorded as part of documentation, a statement the principal made in a letter to teachers, or a close paraphrase of a comment a parent made. That way the quotation is truly coming from the other person and has the sound of a different voice in the story, just as a real interview quote would, but you can get the quote without taking up much time from the source and without listening to the source hem and haw and get shy about saying something for the press.

Of course, before using the quote, check with the source of the quote to make sure you have permission! Many people, especially those who are not used to dealing with the media, will struggle with phrasing or even object to the whole idea when interviewed but are quite content and even proud to see their name in print once they see their own words presented as an expert or eyewitness quote in your news release. It is usually not too difficult to get sources to agree to being quoted in a news release when the work has been done for them.

Tips to make a story newsworthy to local media are listed in Figure 10.2.

Providing Contact Information

Another area where many "amateur" communicators miss the mark is in providing a contact. A news release absolutely must provide a specific individual to contact for more information, and that individual must be reachable during business hours. Furthermore, that person needs to be ready to answer media questions and prepared to be quoted. Do not provide as the contact person someone who will say he or she can't be quoted or doesn't know the answers. If teachers or staff are not permitted or not encouraged to talk to reporters, the contact person should be someone who does have that authority, such as a principal.

News reporters expect to be able to talk to the people directly involved with a story as part of their normal investigation of a story. Doing a story without talking directly to the people involved would be considered bad journalism. Once invited to cover a story, news reporters are free to cover it as they see fit. They are not under the control of educators or any other sources, and this independence makes them valuable to society. When reporters talk to a source, that person must be free to answer questions. Sometimes when people answer an unexpected question on the spot, their phrasing is less than ideal.

Figure 10.2. Tips to make the story more newsworthy.

Tips to Make the Story More Newsworthy

- Tie it in to issues that are already topics of discussion in the public forum. State the link to recent news coverage explicitly—don't expect reporters or their audiences to remember that this is an example of the education issue the legislature has been discussing.

- Emphasize the local angle of the story by mentioning involvement of other local organizations or people. For example, for a story about a project on farms that included a field trip to a local farm, include the name of the local farmer. Businesses, organizations, and people who have helped with the project will appreciate the positive press, too!

- Find a "news angle," something immediate or current, something new or something unusual. This could be an upcoming event, and event that has just occurred (as in today or yesterday), or a new teaching method or curriculum.

- Use quotes and anecdotes to bring your message to life.

- Tell the audience why the issue matters to them and/or how they might get involved.

- Provide visuals, especially photos. Submitted photos should:
  - √ Be close-ups and action shots, not posed group photos.
  - √ Be clearly labeled, including names and, if relevant, titles of anyone recognizable. For minors, you will need parental permission.
  - √ Be in focus and have good contrast—the photo must be clear.

Sources do their best to answer questions, and reporters do their best to quote selectively and make it sound good.

Administrators who are not prepared to relinquish control of news media coverage to reporters and their sources should think twice about inviting the media to cover a story in the first place. It is not possible to reach out to audiences through the media and keep perfect control over the content, style, or audience reaction. Any attempts to control coverage will be seen as attempts to undermine the independence or objectivity of the news media and will likely be met with annoyance at best, anger at worst. Educators' reluctance to talk to the media and avoidance of the media out of fear of saying the wrong thing may protect staff and avoid some minor problems, but it also means the loss of an important communication channel and contributes to societal audiences' lack of understanding of education issues.

Even if the press release contains all the information the reporter needs, many newspapers want to check facts or simply confirm the story with a real person before running it. In general, the more time a reporter spends on a story, the more coverage the story will get. Because they must have audio and/or video footage, broadcast news almost always has to be prepared by a reporter. In print, "real" stories written by a reporter are often treated as more newsworthy than a press release. Press releases may be run deep in the newspaper with minimal editing, but when news media present a story as news, a reporter will probably want to fact-check, do interviews, and customize the writing. Thus, once you've invited the media to cover your story, don't be shy about talking to them when they come around with questions! Their questions are a reflection of their interest in the story and their perception of the importance of the story.

It is not uncommon for reporters to have only a few hours to do a story. How the story turns out, when it runs, or even if it runs at all is often determined by whom reporters can contact and when they can contact them. If a reporter cannot reach a contact person before the story becomes old news, the story may be rejected. For classroom teachers, providing contact information may require some creativity. Provide a home telephone number, a school telephone number, and the times when you can be reached at each. E-mail may help. As previously mentioned, it is a good idea to have a business card with this information on it. Business cards can be included with a press release. You can also provide other contact names and telephone numbers, such as a principal—of course, make sure they are prepared to comment intelligently! Submitting the news release in advance and including the hours you can be reached will help a great deal; even busy reporters are capable of adjusting their schedule to reach key sources if they have some advance notice. Returning calls to news media as promptly as possible is also very important.

Contact information, additional resources, invitations for reporters or photographers to stop by for an activity, and anything else that is intended as notes for reporters and editors and *not* intended to be published as part of the news story should be clearly separated from the body of the story, possibly even on a separate sheet of paper.

Contacts Other Than Press Releases

A press release is a document that the author has released to the press with the expectation that it may appear in print or on a broadcast. The assumption is that everything stated in the press release was approved for release by the author, the sources quoted, and the organization they represent. Things that are not intended for publication should not be in press release format.

Sometimes educators would like to talk to news media without calling for a story. For example, a teacher might want to invite the photographer from the local newspaper to drop in on the class field trip to a local farm. But certainly the public is not to be invited to the field trip. Furthermore, since it is not an event to which the public is invited, it would make more sense to report on the event immediately afterwards. Thus, the teacher does not want a story about the field trip to run beforehand. In this case, a press release is not appropriate. A business letter or fax to the attention of the news editor, education editor, or a specific reporter or photographer is appropriate to notify media in a nonstory format. The basic content of a press release would still need to be addressed. Whether news staff cover the story themselves or rely on a press release or letter, they will be looking for the same things to compose the story: a news angle, the basic facts (who, what, when, where, why and how), interesting points and convincing evidence, and quotations and attributions from several sources.

When inviting news staff to an event, any information the reporter or photographer would need to attend should be included. Do they need directions to a location? Where should they park? If visitors are required to check in at a school office, tell them to check in and tell them where the office is, as well as the room for the event. If news media will be checking in at a school or center office, it is a good idea to tell the office staff to expect them and where to direct them when they come in. If a ticket is needed to get in, tell them how to get around this requirement and make sure your ticket collectors know to let the press in. If it is a long activity, provide some guidance as to when they might capture the best action.

It is okay to talk to reporters and editors informally. The best way to reach out to the media may be to telephone the news editor, education editor, or a specific reporter; explain to them that you thought they might be interested in a particular project or event; find out if they might be interested and how they would like you to help. If they would like to attend, offer to follow up with a written invitation with all the details.

For educators who will likely have several events to share with the media, such as a public library director or a school principal, it is probably a good idea to work on building a relationship. This does not have to be a major project. Find out who covers stories like yours. A news media website or the staff box in the newspaper will often label someone as an education reporter or editor. Even if one has not been labeled, you can look at several newscasts or newspaper editions and figure out who usually covers education issues. Talk to that person about the kinds of stories you have and what would be the best way to let the news staff know about them. Make it clear that you understand that your stories may be soft news and that you do not expect them to cover everything, but you'd like them to know about activities in case they have space or a slow news day. You can also ask them about options for sharing news if a reporter does not cover an activity. For example, would the news staff like for you to bring in a press release and photo after the event? Your contact has a good idea of how interested the news media outlet will be in your news. If they're not interested, this chat will save you a lot of time and prevent you from annoying the news staff by inundating them with information they are unlikely to use. If they are interested, this chat will tell you, far better than this book can, about the particular needs and policies of that media outlet. Before you have this conversation, do your homework. Read, listen, or watch numerous newscasts and get a sense of what they typically cover. When a new reporter comes in, you will have to have this meeting and build the relationship again. Turnover is very high at small news outlets, where reporters and photographers often get experience before moving up to larger outlets.

Being Interviewed by the News Media: Talking Points

Being interviewed by a reporter is not as scary as people might think, especially for a positive, soft-news story. The best way to prepare for an interview is to prepare "talking points." This simply means making a list of points you would like to share. These are usually not in sentence form but rather in note or bullet-point form—this keeps you from reading. When you are being interviewed on television, you need to look as if you are having a natural conversation with someone; of course, you cannot be looking down and reading. For radio, there is no visual element—but listeners can "hear" you looking down and reading. Furthermore, the style of written language is different from that of spoken language. If you write out full-fledged sentences, the language will probably sound overly formal or canned. The best way to make your radio recording, or even your quotations in print, sound natural and conversational is to actually have it be a natural conversation. Keeping your talking points in note or bullet-point form will help you do this.

Talking points should include a list of the main points you want to make and some specific examples you can refer to. It is often difficult to think of an example on the spot—sometimes it seems that all our examples disappear the moment we need them! Therefore, plan your examples in advance. As discussed in Strategy Three, "Convince with Evidence," and Strategy Four, "Plan Your Message," make points for which you have good supporting evidence—good documentation and examples. Choose messages that are relevant for your audience, keep a tight focus, and support your message with evidence that is convincing and powerful.

Talking points are a standard professional communication tool. They can be used for any unstructured, small meeting, such as a parent–teacher conference, or as preparation for an open-house event. For topics that communicators will frequently need to address, talking points can be developed and kept on hand. Teams and organizations can also distribute talking points to members to help people deliver a consistent message. They are frequently used to train political volunteers for meetings with citizens. Chapter 11, Foundation Builders, discusses talking points in more detail.

Before you talk to a reporter, write out your talking points. Having them written down in front of you when you do the interview will help you if you become nervous. If you have contacted a reporter, you know there is a good possibility that reporter will want to talk to you. Have your talking points ready before you submit your press release or other initial contact so that you do not keep the reporter waiting on deadline. If you did not expect to talk to a reporter, it is OK to ask for a brief delay so that you can get organized. When you hear from a reporter, your first question should be, "When is your deadline?" You may have a few days to schedule a time to talk. Even if the deadline is fast approaching, it is okay to ask if you can call back in 15 or 30 minutes—if they can't wait that long, they'll tell you! In most cases, they would rather interview someone who is organized and prepared, so it's worth it to them to wait. For a broadcast, they will probably schedule an appointment to shoot some video, so you will have a little organizing time anyway. Think about the questions you expect the reporter to ask and make sure your talking points cover those topics. Organize your talking points in inverted pyramid style. The interview may be over sooner than you think, so get your key points out early.

Before the interview, also gather up any other materials you would like to refer to. If you plan to share examples of documentation, have them ready. If you have brochures or other background information about your program, school, center, or teaching approach, have those ready. If you plan to discuss a teaching methodology, have articles with research on the approach ready. These will be the additional information, your "jump page" for the interview. Refer to them if it fits naturally in the flow of the interview; if not, offer them at the end as resources for the reporter.

Nowadays, most interviews for print media take place on the phone. If a photograph is planned, that will often be arranged separately with the photographer. Radio interviews can be completed on the phone, at an event, or in the radio recording studio. Television reporters may do some background work on the phone, but at some point they usually need video footage. For a 2 or 3-minute story, they will need several different scenes to shoot. They may pan the camera across children's work, show children in action, or pan the camera around a classroom or show the outside of a building. Sometimes they set up staged video footage; play along if they ask you to pose or walk down a hallway. Trust their judgment about what will look good on camera, but don't be afraid to suggest ideas. For example, you might suggest showing some good documentation on camera.

During the interview, look for opportunities to work in your talking points. Usually this is easy. The process of preparing your talking points will have put those talking points on the tip of your tongue, and most likely the questions fit the talking points anyway. If the interview goes off in a different direction, don't get so focused on your talking points that you don't answer the question as asked. Listen to questions and make sure your answer truly addresses the questions. If you feel that you are not getting to make points you thought were important, it is okay (especially in any interview except live broadcast) to tell the reporter you think this other point is really important.

Often, for a positive news story, the reporter's main goal is to give you an opportunity to tell your story and to capture you telling your story in your own words in video footage, audiotape, or a quotation. The reporter is not trying to stump you, but rather to ask questions that will bring out your story and help you elaborate on details. The reporter may also be looking for ways to make your story seem relevant and significant to readers. Thus, you can expect the reporter to ask you why things are important, how activities relate to skills and outcomes later in life. Prepare your talking points so that you have something to say, including interesting and meaningful examples and documentation.

Sometimes reporters ask questions that are really designed get you to talk—the reporters may even know the answers themselves. What they want is to get your answer in your own words. Don't give yes or no answers; rather, try to answer in complete sentences and offer extra information and details. If the goals of your new program were stated in your press release and the reporter asks you the goal of your program, don't jump to the conclusion that the reporter didn't bother to read the release. Instead, the reporter probably knows the goals and is trying to give you an opportunity to summarize the main purpose in your own, natural-sounding words, not some formal goal statement. Reporters want you to talk; help them out. Look at the reporters' questions as opportunities.

They will also ask questions in order to find out answers. Again, they are not quizzing you or trying to stump you. Answer as best as you can. Don't panic if you don't know. If you don't know the answers, say so. If appropriate, you can suggest someone who might know the answer or offer to try to find out.

For print media, doing an interview is just like a conversation. The reporter will ask questions and the source will answer. Your "umm's" and "uhh's" and grammatical errors (which happen to the best of us in conversational speech) will all be edited out when they write up the quotations. Comments you made that were not quotable will be paraphrased in the reporter's own succinct language. Reporters try to make expert sources sound like experts. They do not want their sources to look stupid! They will work with your words to make them as coherent and interesting as possible without changing them. At the interview stage, for print reporters, more is better. Give the reporter something to work with, and he or she can edit to select the best parts.

For broadcast media, doing an interview is also a conversation, but broadcast media must use your actual audio or video recording. It is much harder for them to edit out "umm's" and grammatical errors, and they need at least a few coherent, unbroken statements.

They also need places to cut. Speaking in short, but complete, sentences makes it easier for them to edit. Some broadcast interviews are even live, which means the news staff have no opportunity to help you out with their professional editing. This means that for broadcast media, interview subjects need to work hard to speak in short, complete sentences and avoid "umm's" and mistakes, while still making eye contact and looking and sounding natural. Broadcast news segments are very, very short, usually only a few minutes. The interviewer is used to managing this short time frame. Follow his or her lead to make sure you get the basic information covered quickly. For a broadcast, less is more. No matter how short you try to keep it, you may still feel like you were cut off too soon. For a broadcast interview, it may be helpful to actually write out some short, conversational sentences, or "sound bites," in your talking points. Though you do not want to read them during the interview, phrasing them in advance may help you phrase them smoothly on camera.

For people who are not used to being on television, the natural tendency is to worry a lot about how they look on television. Dress professionally and avoid clothes that are distracting—remember that professionalism builds credibility. But, as with most communications, what you say is more important. The important thing is to get your point across coherently.

Timing

Time moves with lightening speed in the news industry. Yesterday's news is nothing today and completely forgotten tomorrow. We might wax philosophical about the disadvantages of this attitude, but it remains a fact that people who want to work through media will have to deal with. It is not uncommon for "amateur" communicators from local nonprofit organizations to bring in a press release a week after the event when an officer got around to it. By then, it is old news. If they are lucky, it might be run in the back pages of a very small newspaper strictly as a community service; broadcast media have no back pages, so it would likely be ignored altogether. If the release had been brought in the day after the activity, it might have been placed on the front page, or at least the front page of the local section. If reporters had been told about it before the event, they might have covered it themselves.

News media need to know about your story immediately, on the same day as the event or possibly the next day if the event was late in the day. If you are submitting photos, this means getting 1-hour film development and dropping the photos and press release off later the same day as the event. It's a good idea to check with the media outlet before you go to this trouble—staff will be happy to tell you whether they are interested and what they would like brought in. Digital is another option. Keep in mind that only photos taken with the highest-resolution setting on your camera will likely be acceptable. If you are inviting them to attend, they need a week or at least a few days notice to schedule. For a weekly publication, check with a receptionist for advice about timing—normally schedules are more relaxed than for a daily, but a 1-day delay on the wrong day could mean a week's delay in publication, and by then your item might not be sufficiently new to get in at all.

THE NEXT STEP

Now that the strategies are understood, it is time to go from learning to doing. To begin the process, go to Part III, where forms and directions are located. It is time to begin to gather that documentation and open some windows.

Resources for Educator-Communicators

CHAPTER 11

Foundation Builders:
Resources for Thinking Strategically

WHY THINK STRATEGICALLY?

ONE OF THE WAYS THAT professional communicators accomplish their goals is to communicate *strategically*. In strategic communication, the communicator consciously recognizes communication goals and consciously designs the messages to increase the likelihood of achieving those goals, including goals not explicitly stated in the message. Only by strategically designing communication can an education organization hope to take full advantage of a communication opportunity.

To be an effective communicator, it is important to build a foundation for strategic communication within your organization. This includes:

- Understanding your audience
- Identifying your credible communicators
- Providing support to your communicators

In this chapter you will find forms to assist you in these tasks.

WHO CAN USE FOUNDATION BUILDERS?

If you are a member of a team, a school faculty, a school district, or an educational organization, and if your team is on board you can use the following pages as a group. An administrator or director can serve as a leader or if there is a communications professional on staff, he or she may want to set up a series of meetings in

which groups work together to make these decisions. If a school within a larger organization decides to do this, then, of course, anyone responsible for professional communications within the organization should be included. The benefits of strategic communication are multiplied when the message is consistent and everyone speaks with one voice.

If you are alone, you will still find it beneficial to think through this process. A classroom teacher or an educator working alone, such as a community art instructor, can use the following pages to think through his or her own communication goals and strategies.

DOING THE BUILDING

Putting in place a strong foundation for powerful communication using student work takes some effort. The forms on the following pages can be copied and completed during a 1-day retreat or a series of meetings by a faculty or group of educators.

1. *Audience analysis, including the following:*
   Demographics
   Psychographics
   Benefits and usage
2. *Identification of communication goals*
3. *Development of talking points about important issues that can be used when speaking to the press, addressing a group of parents, or writing an article*
4. *Formal statements endorsed by a group*

5. *Analysis of supports in place for using documentation for communication, including the following:*
   Access to technology
   Technology training
   Budget for PR materials
   Communication resources available in teacher
      resource library
   Permission slips for photos
   Practicum students or observers

The audience should be the first consideration of communication. Thus, we suggest that audience analysis be one of the first foundation-building activities for strategic communication planning. The process of audience analysis is explained in Strategy One, "Analyze Your Audience." Reproducible worksheets are provided on pages 100–102 to guide educator-communicators through the process of analyzing their audiences with respect to demographics, psychographics, benefits, and usage.

The next step in building a foundation is deciding what to say at a big-picture level. On pages 103–104, we provide two reproducible worksheets, one on communication goals and one on developing a message calendar, to guide this part of the strategic communication planning process.

Once you've set communication goals, you may be able to further flesh out key messages by planning talking points and preparing formal statements to share with key audiences.

TALKING POINTS

What Are Talking Points?

As discussed in Strategy Seven, "Reach Out to the Media," talking points are simply a list of points to make in an unstructured discussion, such as an interview with a reporter or a parent–teacher conference. Like notes a person would prepare for a speech, talking points summarize key information in note or bullet-point form, avoiding crafting carefully worded statements or paragraphs. This keeps the focus on the content of the message rather than the language and leaves speakers free to use spontaneous, natural, conversational language in their own styles. Unlike notes for a speech, talking points are intended to be used in less structured, conversational meetings or interactions. Also unlike notes for a speech, talking points are primarily a preparation tool and are meant to be very flexible. They help orga-

nize thoughts and remind speakers of the points they intended to work into the natural conversation. Anyone can prepare informal talking points for any specific communication event. A teacher might jot some notes on points she wants to cover before she picks up the telephone to call a parent to discuss a child. The notes help her keep the conversation on track and ensure she doesn't forget an important point.

Formal Talking Points

Professional communicators often prepare more formal talking points for important messages that will be addressed repeatedly. The talking points reflect a communication strategy for getting a key message across. Individuals can develop formal talking points as part of a communication strategy and can refer to the talking points for a quick reminder of key messages in future communications. For teams, this process offers the additional benefit of helping the team agree on communication strategy so that messages can be delivered consistently. The process of developing talking points can be as valuable as the outcome. Because talking points focus on content, not language, individual members of the team will still present the message naturally in their own way. Educators can use this process to prepare talking points on key issues for their programs.

Possible Topics for Formal Talking Points

- Philosophy of school or program
- Curriculum methods
- Achievement of students
- Need for parent participation
- Value of community participation
- New methodology or approach
- New organization or program

Directions

1. *Identify key audiences* with whom educators might be talking about this issue.
2. Discuss audience members' likely background knowledge, attitudes, and information needs on the issue. Review your audience analysis. *Brainstorm a list of audience needs and concerns about this issue.*
3. *Brainstorm a list of key main points* and put them on index cards or Post-it notes. (If working with a team, team members can brainstorm on their

own and then share.) Combine redundant main points and/or group-proposed points into main points and supporting points. Keep the focus on content, not phrasing. Focus on which messages you want to get across to the audience rather than on particular evidence or references.

4. *Prioritize the points* and arrange them in inverted pyramid style (see Strategy Four, "Plan Your Message," for details on inverted pyramid style). In real, unstructured conversations, you won't necessarily make these points in this order. But points at the top will get more emphasis. When possible, you can try to get the top points across first.

5. Look again at your list of audience needs and concerns. How does your list of talking points look so far? *Revise to better meet audience needs and your communication goals.*

6. *Add supporting points and evidence to the main points.* Individuals using the talking points (i.e., individuals talking to people about this issue) can supply their own evidence in the future. For example, teachers would naturally want to use recent examples of documentation from their own classrooms. However, including *some* sample supporting points and evidence with the talking points means speakers will have at least a few valid examples on hand as a starting point, and coming up with examples together can help the team get a sense of what kinds of examples they might use. Consider which kinds of support or evidence are most powerful for the audience. What have team members learned from reactions in previous conversations on the topic? What was most powerful for team members themselves when first learning about the issue?

7. *Add references.* While educators will likely use their own examples and anecdotes, it may be helpful for teams and organizations to agree on key references to cite. These could include books on particular teaching methods, articles on model schools, or articles with research results supporting the teaching method. For teams, it's a good idea to make sure key communicators have copies of these references on hand and have read them. Adding references can be as simple as agreeing on a leading book on the teaching methodology, which most of the team members have probably already read anyway, and taking the trouble to get the citation right and include it in the talking points. In conversations, you won't exactly cite a

source. But if someone asks if there's any research showing that the method works, the answer is ready. Or if someone is especially interested, it is easy to refer them to a good book on the subject. Preparing and reviewing the talking points' references will also make speakers more familiar with them—and thus more likely to refer to them in ordinary conversation. "Actually, I read this article that shows children have better comprehension with this approach . . ."

8. Now, just briefly, *consider language.* Check to see if there are any potential language problems: Are educators using jargon that audience members won't understand? Are educators using phrasing that could be offensive to any audience members? Limit this discussion to phrasing team members use among themselves but don't want to use with the audience. Avoid getting picky about other phrasing so that speakers will be free to speak naturally. Revise your talking points into audience-appropriate language. Consider printing key terms in boldface or italics. For example, boldface could be a reminder for speakers that a particular term is education jargon and that they might want to avoid it or explain it. Individual speakers can use their own judgment as to what's appropriate for the particular people they are talking with.

9. *Reach a final consensus on your talking points.* Make arrangements to distribute the final copy of the talking points to team members. If appropriate, make arrangements to share your team's talking points with professional communication staff or a principal or director. Talk about ways you will use them.

10. *Use the talking points to talk to audiences.* Review the talking points before events when talking about the issue is likely. Keep the talking points and audience analysis in mind during spontaneous conversations on the issue.

11. *Use the talking points to talk to education partners and build team consistency.* Share the talking points with aides, volunteers, and new team members.

FORMAL STATEMENTS

From Talking Points to Formal Statements

The talking points developed in the previous exercise can be a starting point for developing more formal statements. Talking points are a tool for clarifying message content. They are meant to be read by the educator-communicators who use them, not by audiences. The next step is to put that message content into written form so that audiences can read it independently. This activity can be used by a team or an individual educator.

Why Create Formal Statements?

Any topic that educators need to explain repeatedly and consistently can be addressed in some kind of formal statement, that is, a document that can be circulated and shared with multiple audiences. Topics such as those we listed for talking points are suitable. Example documents might include program mission statements, brochures explaining teaching methods, handouts, or fact sheets. These documents are time savers for educator-communicators. They provide a convenient, professional-looking summary of key issues. A single trifold brochure summarizing a center's teaching approach can be provided to prospective parents as a marketing tool and to new parents as an orientation, set out at public events in case visitors need background information, displayed along with teachers' work at conferences as a convenient summary of the context, included with press releases to provide background for media, shared with business sponsors, and shared with other educators such as after-school care programs. Once such a brochure has been prepared, educator-communicators can make this background information available as optional additional information for any audience in any communication situation simply by getting a few copies out of a file.

Directions

1. *Plan your message.* Content comes first! If you've already completed the talking points exercise, you can use your talking points as your message plan. If not, complete the talking points exercise as a planning tool.
2. *Take talking points step 6, add supporting points and evidence to the main points, to a higher level.* In the talking points development process, you thought about types of documentation that would be effective and a few examples to get talking points users started thinking of their own examples. Now you want to strategically choose specific examples to incorporate in the formal document. Review potential documentation to include. Individual members of teams working together

on this project may wish to gather their favorite documentation materials to bring to a team meeting or submit documentation items to an individual or committee in charge of preparing the formal statements. Educators working alone may want to spread out documentation pieces they are considering. Work to match up the best pieces of documentation with the points you want to make.

3. *Select documentation that*
   - Effectively conveys the point
   - Is convincing and powerful
   - Will reproduce well using the intended copying method
   - Is representative of program staff, participants, and learning activities: Does the combination of documentation selected for the formal document show the different age levels, ethnic groups, teachers, and kinds of learning served by the program?
   - The program has permission to use or can get permission to use
4. Take talking points step 7, add references, to a higher level (if appropriate). For example, discussions of teaching philosophies and methods should include a few citations to illustrate a professional basis for the approach and research evidence of its success if possible.
   - If there are relevant specific facts or quotes that can serve as convincing and powerful evidence for the points you want to make, incorporate those as citations. Cited references can be listed as a footnote.
   - If specific citations are not convincing and powerful, you can still build credibility by putting a few references in a For More Information section.
   - If your formal statement refers to, quotes from, or summarizes larger internal documents, the larger documents can be cited as references.
   - Full academic citation style is not necessary.
5. *Prepare a draft document,* including the documentation and art. The team has already agreed on basic content when completing the talking points activity. One member may efficiently prepare a rough draft by putting the talking points into formal document form and incorporating the selected documentation and references. Then the team can revise it.
6. *Revise the draft document.* Educators working alone still need to view revision as a step in the process.

It's best to let it sit for a day or two, then revise. Educators working alone may also want to get a friend to proofread the document before printing and/or ask a principal, director, or colleague for feedback. Fresh eyes can spot problems authors overlook! During the revision process, teams and individuals should look for

- Relevant messages and tight focus
- Good writing—make it interesting
- Audience-appropriate language and phrasing
- Use of language and phrasing that will be clear to the least informed audience and not offensive to any audiences if the document will be used for multiple audiences.
- Professional tone
- Relevant contact information (e.g., as part of a letterhead or in small print on the back of a brochure) so that anyone looking at your document will know where to find you.
- Good use of design principles (contrast, repetition, alignment, and proximity)

7. *Make arrangements to have the final version prepared.* Plan how you will use the document, how to distribute it, and how many to produce.
8. *Get approvals* from administrators if necessary.
9. *Have it printed or make copies yourself.* Make sure arrangements have been made to easily print additional copies and revise.
10. *Distribute* to team members and use. Also distribute multiple copies to education partners who might pass them on to others.

Design Tips for Formal Statements

- Follow the design principles of contrast, repetition, alignment, and proximity.
- Use headings, subheadings, and bullet points—this organizes the information for your reader and adds visual interest
- Use a trifold brochure or booklet format to make your document stand out as a handy reference. If you use an 8½" × 11" page size format, use letterhead and a two- or three-column layout to make

it look more formal and professional. These formatting cues, made easy by Microsoft Publisher, signal your audience that this is a formal statement, a handy reference to keep.

- Avoid clip-art. Instead, break up text with children's work from your program, photos of children actively engaged in learning in your program, figures or charts, or and/or pull-out quotes that help communicate the message. Your graphics should have meaning and enhance or support your message, not distract from it.
- Print in black on distinctive paper to dress up your document without breaking your budget. For an inexpensive but professional look, go for standard-quality paper in a neutral color — beige, gray, ivory, yellow, pale blue, or green. For a more upscale look at a slightly higher price, go for resume-style paper with subtle visual texture such as granite, marble, or parchment.
- Experiment with photos and artwork to make sure they will reproduce well on a copier if you plan to photocopy your document.
- Limit the color, if you can afford color, to documentation artwork and photos to maximize the impact. Keep the focus on student learning!
- Customize the document, if possible. For example, a one-third sheet mini-brochure with an individual teacher's background, photo, and philosophy could be inserted into a center's trifold brochure on the program philosophy, or a similar insert for a specific grade level could be added to a brochure on an assessment system.

The following pages provide templates which may be photocopied and used by educator-communicators as worksheets to aid in laying a foundation for strategic communication. Worksheets cover audience analysis (demographics, psychographics, benefits, and usage), identification of communication goals, developing a message calendar, and a checklist for determining whether your program provides sufficient support to encourage strategic communication.

DEMOGRAPHICS

Directions: Many schools have these data for their community. Other educational institutions may get these from libraries. Some of the data can also be found on entry forms or gathered by observation. Taking time to summarize and think of implications will help make communication more meaningful.

Demographic	Most of My Families	Some of My Families	Communication Implications
Educational Level			
Language			
Ethnic Background			
Ages of Parents			
Age Groups of Children in Home			
Family Structure			
Job Schedules			

PSYCHOGRAPHICS

Directions: To understand the psychographics of your audience talk to them about their lifestyles, use questionnaires, and be sure to have representatives of different cultures on your governing boards. Get to know families and the community.

Psychographic	Most of My Families	Some of My Families	Communication Implications
Identification with Ethnicity			
Lifestyle			
Religion			
Values			
Other			

BENEFITS AND USAGE ANALYSIS

Directions: Understanding how your communication audience sees the benefits of your educational program and thinking about how the program fits into their lives enables you to better understand how they will interpret your communication.

	Most of My Families	*Some of My Families*	*Communication Implications*
How much do they use the center or school?			
What do they see as the primary purpose of the center or school in their lives?			
What do they see as benefits of choosing this center or school over others?			

COMMUNICATION GOALS

Directions: After completing the audience analysis worksheets on the preceding pages, consider the implications of demographics, psychographics, and the benefits and usage analysis for communication. List communication goals for the next year for the following groups. Work through the questions in the Seeing the Big Picture section in Strategy Four: "Plan Your Message."

Our Communication Goals

Communication with our families?

Communication with the members of our community?

Communication with supervisory or advisory groups or individuals (parent advisory board, school board, principal)?

MESSAGE CALENDAR

Directions: A message calendar is a planning tool used to deliver parts of a message over a long period of time or different approaches or channels for a message over a period of time. Example: Focus—Learning experiences in our schools match state standards. A different area of learning will be highlighted each month. After listing communication goals based on audience needs (previous worksheet), review the goals list. If necessary, break communication goals down into smaller bite-sized messages. For example, if the overall goal is to demonstrate that state standards are being met, that goal could be broken down into separate messages for each topic area of the curriculum. Next, consider documentation that could be used to support those messages and channels that might be appropriate, and then consider a tentative time frame. As you plan a time frame for each message, think about other things that will be going on at that time in your program, in the school or community, or in people's lives generally, and how those activities might impact their interests and concerns. Message calendars are further discussed in Strategy Four: "Plan Your Message."

Defined Focus		
Messages for Each Time Period (State in a Sentence)	*Documentation We Can Use (Brainstorm Most Powerful)*	*List Time Frame for the Calendar (Monthly, Weekly, Quarterly, Ongoing, or Whatever Time Period)*

SUPPORT ANALYSIS

Directions: The following list of materials and resources can be used to assess the support available to the credible or frontline communicators in an educational program. Resources and training can then be planned and put into budgets.

1. Access to technology
   - ☐ Computer with desktop publishing software such as Microsoft Publisher
   - ☐ Scanner
   - ☐ Color printer
   - ☐ Digital camera (quick and easy access)
   - ☐ Digital video camera (not necessary but helpful)
   - ☐ Photocopy machine
   - ☐ Presentation software such as PowerPoint
   - ☐ Tape recorder for recording discussions
   - ☐ Web space for classroom updates and documentation

2. Training available
   - ☐ Desktop publishing—easy program such as Microsoft Publisher
   - ☐ Presentation software
   - ☐ Preparation of documentation panels and displays
   - ☐ Website updating
   - ☐ Collection of documentation of student work

3. Resources available
   - ☐ Templates for displays, talking points, press releases
   - ☐ Books on documentation display
   - ☐ Permission forms for photos, student work, and teacher work to be used in displays and publications
   - ☐ Access to books and resource materials on display, design, and newsletters by professionals for non-professionals

4. Budget for public relations materials
   - ☐ Color ink and paper for printing photos
   - ☐ Funds for enlarging documentation panels in black and white if not available within institution
   - ☐ Newsletter funds
   - ☐ Frames or foam core boards for displaying documentation panels in the community
   - ☐ Brochures and background papers

CHAPTER 12

Tools for Opening Windows: Looking Professional

THE CHALLENGE FOR MANY EDUCATORS in communicating professionally is the time and effort required. In this chapter, we tried to do some of the work for you so that you can concentrate on your message. One of the ways to reduce time and effort is to develop tools that you can use again and again. This section includes

- A model for a press release about a learning experience or event (pp. 110–111)
- A checklist for submitting photos and art (pp. 106–107)
- Directions for developing a desktop publishing template for displays of student work (pp. 107–109)
- Two inverted pyramid diagrams for organizing a message or display (pp. 113–114)

The last tool we share with you is a list of resources that are helpful in learning more about communication, graphic design, digital photography, and other information that will help you become a better communicator.

SUBMITTING PHOTOS AND ARTWORK TO THE MEDIA

Including photographs of children working and their work will help educator-communicators get their message out. These photos and art can offer convincing and powerful evidence of children's learning to reporters and editors. If those reporters and editors choose to publish or broadcast that documentation, their au-diences will also have the opportunity to share in the excitement of student learning.

Including photographs or other art also increases the likelihood that a press release will get media attention and news time or space. Journalists often use the term *art* to include anything that is not text—photos, drawings, diagrams, and charts. Television news staff are always looking for visual images, and print journalists are always looking for art to break up the text as a layout tool. Including art means your press release package is more complete—less work for news staff. Of course, pictures cannot be shown on radio, but you can include them anyway because they increase reporters' interest in and understanding of the story. They are convincing, and educator-communicators want media staff to be convinced of the truth and importance of their message!

Radio news staff are always looking for interesting audio. Television can pan across still images, but TV reporters are always looking for video to accompany a story. If you have documentation that is in audio or video format, mention it on your release. If they are interested, broadcast news staff will handle the technical details.

Checklist for submitting photographs and art
- Show close-ups of children in action.
- Have good contrast and good focus.
- If photos are digital, use high resolution. Submit a good printout of the digital photo, and either provide or offer to provide the electronic copy.

Print the photo at 100%, or actual size. Prints from film are fine, too.

- Provide a digital photo or a clean color or black-and-white photocopy of children's work. Don't submit originals. If possible, have the original on hand for news staff to borrow.
- Provide a caption that tells more about what is happening in the photo. Use the caption to interpret the moment or the work for the viewer in order to provide meaning. Don't state the obvious, and don't say "This shows. . . ."
- In the caption, identify anyone who is recognizable in the photo.
- For photos of children, provide signed permission slips for their use or note that the school or program has such permission slips on file. You also need such permission slips for children's work.
- Provide only one or two photos. But you can provide thumbnails of other art available or list audio and video material you have available.

TEMPLATES FOR DISPLAY: USING DESKTOP PUBLISHING AND ENLARGING FOR PANELS

Creating Displays

Creating attractive displays can be time consuming and expensive. Professional communicators create displays using software and print them on paper or canvas using large-format color printers. Or they may have especially prepared portable displays to which they add features. Most of these are not in the budget or within expertise of educational programs. However, displays do not have to be limited to looking like bulletin board or science projects. Attractive displays can be created that are not time consuming or extremely expensive using a simple desktop publishing program, a personal color printer, and the enlargement capabilities of a local photocopying business, such as Kinko's.

Most of the displays that appear in this book were created in this manner by educator-communicators using templates on a desktop publishing program. These were then printed in black and white and enlarged to display size on a poster maker or a large-format photo copier. Some were printed directly on large-format printers at a photocopying business. Large school districts sometimes have large-format printers in design departments or teacher resource centers. If you are going to have the displays printed directly in large format,

be sure to get a price quote. Printing them in black and white will cost less than $5; printing them in color will sometimes cost as much as $100. For an inexpensive way to accomplish a professional-looking display, we print the display in black and white, then print photos and children's work using color printers. We then fasten them to the display using double-stick tape.

By having our panels printed on flexible paper about 2" larger than the actual display area, we can wrap them around the edges of foam core boards or cardboard. They can then be hung, placed on easels, or even framed easily.

Using Templates

The use of desktop publishing for creating displays can be simplified for educators by providing templates that can be made available on networks and on websites for downloading. We have found the following benefits to the use of templates and photo enlarging:

- Professional-looking displays can be created quickly.
- Displays can be changed and targeted for different groups simply by printing different versions.
- New copies can be printed easily to keep the appearance new.
- Emphasis is more on content and less on display.
- Displays can be printed on 8½" × 11" or 8½" × 14" paper and given to parents, students, and others.
- Smaller versions can be placed in documentation albums as an archive of achievements.
- Archives are easier to maintain because displays can be removed and rolled up or simply saved in digital format.
- Educator-communicators learn the principles of good design, and then become more creative as their skills increase.

Creating Templates

Templates can be created in any desktop publishing software. The following guidelines are what have worked for us through trial and error:

Setting page size and margins

1. Choose legal (8½" × 14") or letter (8½" × 11") paper size—landscape (horizontal) or portrait (vertical) orientation. Keeping to a standard paper size simplifies the use.
2. Set ¾" top and side margins, and a 1" margin on the bottom.

Working with text frames

1. Each frame is made separately to enable the user to move the frames around the page to get the most pleasing arrangement.
2. Text sizes and type fonts that we have found work best for enlargement by 200 to 300% are:
   Main Title: Arial 24, boldface
   Subtitle: Arial 18, Roman
   Text: Times New Roman 8, Roman
   Captions: Arial or Times New Roman 9, italic
3. Put placeholder notes (which will be deleted later) into the frames about what works well for communication (see template on page 112).
4. Provide a number of each type of frame so the user can simply drag and drop the frames as needed. In Microsoft Publisher these can appear outside the page margins on the virtual artboard. Each frame should be correctly set up with font and size.

Photos and children's work

Process for digital photos or scanned versions of prints and children's work:

1. Add a photo and children's work to your template to show the appropriate size. (Check the user's manual that came with the software for instructions on how to place art in your document.) Users will need to know how to scan children's work and photos and to put digital photos into a file format which the software will accept.
2. Remind users to crop photos to give them the most meaning (see Strategy Six, "Follow Design Conventions"). Users may need to use a separate photo-editing program, such as Adobe Photoshop, to crop photos.
3. Once the photos are placed in the template, users can move photos around the page to experiment with arrangements and what they want to say.

Process using prints and real children's work:

1. Users will make an empty box for each photo or piece of children's work, making sure to carefully measure the dimensions of each piece of art and size the picture boxes appropriately.
2. Use the empty boxes to do the layout and text and captions

Warning: If the users plan to print photos or children's work on a color printer, they can't make the picture or work any larger than the printer can print, *or* any larger than the size of the photo paper—usually 8½" × 11". That means that the photo on the template cannot be any larger than 4" × 5¼" for a 200% increase. For a 300% increase, it can't be any larger than 2½" × 3½" on the template.

Paragraphs of explanation and captions

1. Provide text frames for paragraphs. Remind users to *spellcheck!*
2. Provide caption frames to go with each picture.
3. Save the file!

Using the Template

Users can print the completed panel out on a desktop printer and then have that paper enlarged to 200% at an office print store or on a large-format copier. For the best quality, the user can have it printed on a large-format printer. When using a large-format printer, talk to the operators of the large-format printer about how they will do that. *Do not agree to print in color unless you know the price first!* If you are in a university, a company, or a large school system, there may be large-format printers in another department that you may use.

Making Your Pictures

A very professional-looking display can be made by printing color photos on a small color printer and then placing these over the black-and-white enlarged versions on your large printed display.

1. Measure the size of the photos on your large printed display. This is the size that each picture will have to be.
2. Adjust the photo or scanned student work and then print it on a color printer. Cut these out using a paper cutter, not scissors, and place them on the panel using tape or glue. If the display will be stored rolled up, then stick the photos on lightly with removable tape, so they can be removed before the display is rolled.
3. Be sure to print out small copies for parents, students, and portfolios. These can be printed in black-and-white or color ink.

Template Model

On page 112 is a model of a template for a display. This page shows what a template would look like when the user opens the template and begins to work with it. Ready-to-use Microsoft Publisher templates may be downloaded from the author's website: *bestpracticesinc.net.*

USING THE INVERTED PYRAMID

The inverted pyramid as described in Strategy Four, "Plan Your Message," can be a time saver for structuring communication messages. On pages 113 and 114 are diagrams that can be used to remind educator-communicators of the inverted pyramid for communication and how to structure messages.

They are designed in poster format so they can be placed near workstations or desks where they are easily accessible.

RECOMMENDED RESOURCES

Software

Microsoft Publisher. Microsoft Publisher is a desktop publisher for amateurs. It is very user-friendly and inexpensive. It offers loads of templates; preformatted blank pages for business cards, brochures, and booklets; design schemes with coordinated fonts and graphic elements; and, for the ultimate in user-friendly help, "wizards" that take you step-by-step through the process of making a document. Word processors are designed for long blocks of text. Desktop publishing software is designed to make it easy to lay out a page or display with text boxes, photos, captions, multiple columns, lines, and boxes.

Adobe Photoshop Elements. The leading photo-editing software for professional communicators and designers is Adobe Photoshop. Adobe offers Photoshop Elements for the rest of us. Besides a full range of photo editing tools, Photoshop Elements includes a versatile photo album system. A single photo can be tagged in multiple ways, making it easy to pull up all the documentation on a particular project, a particular child, or a particular skill or curriculum goal.

Books on Documentation

Helm, J. H., Beneke, S., & Steinheimer, K. (1998). *Windows on learning: Documenting children's work.* New York: Teachers College Press.

This leading book on documentation discusses how documentation can be used to enrich the learning process and provides practical methods for getting started with documentation in the classroom.

Helm, J. H., Beneke, S., & Steinheimer, K. (1998). *Teacher materials for documenting children's work.* New York: Teachers College Press.

This book accompanies *Windows on Learning* and includes supplementary templates and worksheets for a step-by-step guide to getting started documenting in the classroom.

Books on Communication and Design

Williams, R. (2003). *The non-designers design book: Design and typographic principles for the visual novice (2nd ed.).* Berkeley, CA: Peachpit Press.

Robin Williams' insightful book can be read in an afternoon and change the way you think about design. Applying her few simple principles can immediately make your communications more effective.

Grotta, D., & Grotta, S. W. (2004). *PC Magazine guide to digital photography.* Indianapolis, IN: Wiley.

Karlins, D. (2004). *PC Magazine guide to printing great digital photos.* Indianapolis, IN: Wiley.

These two books provide everything you need to know about going digital with your photography. Easy to read, they cover basic information but also information that your manuals buried on the back pages. They can makes a big difference in your photos!

Meek, A. (1999). *Communicating with the public: A guide for school leaders.* Alexandria, VA: Association for Supervision and Curriculum Development.

For educators who want to develop a comprehensive communication and public relations plan for a school or program, this book provides a practical guide.

The Associated Press Stylebook (2005). New York: Associated Press.

This reference book is the "bible" for journalists and public relations professionals. In a dictionary-like format, it provides guidelines for everything from proper formats for attributions and dates to the right way to refer to the federal Education Department. It also includes guidelines for writing a news story and a briefing on media law. The widely used print version includes a punctuation guide; the more narrowly focused broadcast version includes abbreviations and formats for writing broadcast script.

Order online: *http://www.apstylebook.com/*

SCHOOL OR PROGRAM LETTERHEAD

Address, telephone, website, etc. as part of the letterhead

NEWSLIKE HEADLINE TELLS WHAT HAPPENED

For immediate release
Month, day, year

CITY, STATE – Lead: Try to cover the basic Ws (who, what, when, and where) if possible, and tell editors the news angle for your story.

The second sentence usually goes in a separate paragraph, leaving the lead by itself. The second sentence should tell the rest of the Ws (why and how) and summarize why your story is important.

Try to show your news angle in Sentences 1 and 2. News angles can include local events that just (as in today or last night) happened, local events that will happen, something unusual or new, or something with significant local impact. Sometimes if an issue is "hot," or being widely discussed in the national media, comments from local experts or local people affected can be considered newsworthy. For example, when a policy change on Head Start funding is being discussed in the national media, comments from a local school district might be of interest to local media outlets.

The remaining paragraphs provide details of your story in inverted pyramid style – most important main point, most important support for Point 1, Point 2, most important support for Point 2, Point 3, most important support for Point 3, remaining details and support, etc.

As discussed in Strategy Three, "Convince with Evidence," professional communicators want convincing, powerful evidence and support from multiple credible sources. Documentation of children's work can be convincing and powerful evidence. Submitting photos of children engaged in a learning moment and photos of their work will add interest to your story. Be sure to include meaningful captions that interpret the documentation.

Remember that a press release is a news article released to the media for publication. The "For Immediate Release" statement at the top is customary. Almost all press releases are "For Immediate Release."

Press Release Template

Also note other formatting issues. Double-spacing leaves room for editing marks. The date is included at the top. Extra pages show the page number and number of pages. "Slug" is journalism jargon for a short nickname for the story. For example, in a story with the headline "District 10 to Add Preschool Program," the slug could be "Add Preschool," and the header for extra pages would say "Add Preschool, page 2 of 2." ### at the bottom signals the end.

The news release should be short, preferably shorter than 400 words. (This template is 400 words.) Paragraphs are also very short and simple. Try to write for a 4th-grade reading level.

#

Contact Information:
You must list at least one specific person, his or her title, and telephone number.
You might list other contacts as well, and/or alternative phone numbers and e-mail addresses. Make sure editors or reporters can reach someone.

Additional Resources:
Here you can provide a list of other relevant documents you've included, such as a brochure on the center or teaching method or a copy of an article about a new curriculum. You can also list photos or artwork you've included and/or mention that you have photos, artwork, references books, or other materials on hand for reporters.

Upcoming Events:
Here you can mention anything you are inviting reporters or photographers to attend. Details can be provided on a separate sheet.

Margin on top and sides at least ¾"

Arial 24 Bold XXX XXXX XX XXXXX XXX

(Main title—Make title count! 1 to 10 words—raise interest. Could be a question.)

Arial 18 Subtitle here—communicate main idea of your display

(Explain the panel—main idea—10 to 20 words—what you want them to remember.)

Times New Roman 9

Paragraphs—keep this short—no more than 75 words for each paragraph. May do a series of paragraphs.

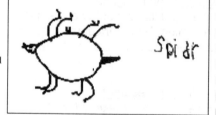

Arial 9 Italics or Plain Captions—give more information than in photo in 10 to 20 words. Match to photo width.

Photos or children's work that is to be printed on a standard color printer to go on an enlarged copy of this display cannot be any larger than the color printer can print. That means that the photo on your template cannot appear any larger than 4" × 5 ¼" for a 200% increase. For a 300% increase it can't be any larger than 2.5" × 3.5" on your screen.

Forms for teacher reflections—make sure to point them inward—What did you learn? What do you want the viewer to remember?

Leave margin of 1" on bottom

The Journalistic Pyramid Applied to Class Newsletters and Letters Home

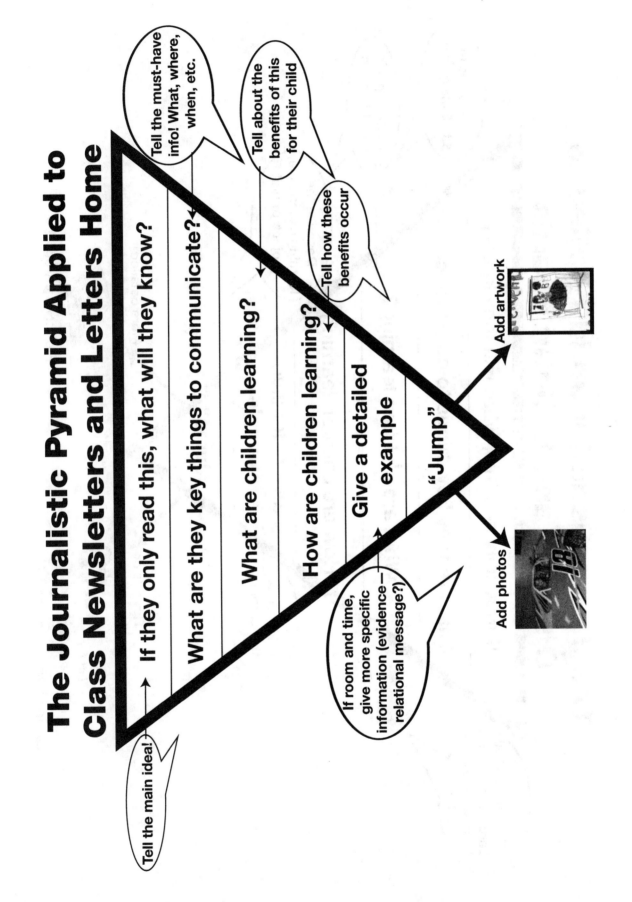

Tell the main idea!

If they only read this, what will they know?

Tell the must-have info! What, where, when, etc.

What are they key things to communicate?

Tell about the benefits of this for their child

What are children learning?

Tell how these benefits occur

How are children learning?

Give a detailed example

"Jump"

If room and time, give more specific information (evidence—relational message?)

Add artwork

Add photos

The Journalistic Pyramid Applied to Displays and Bulletin Boards

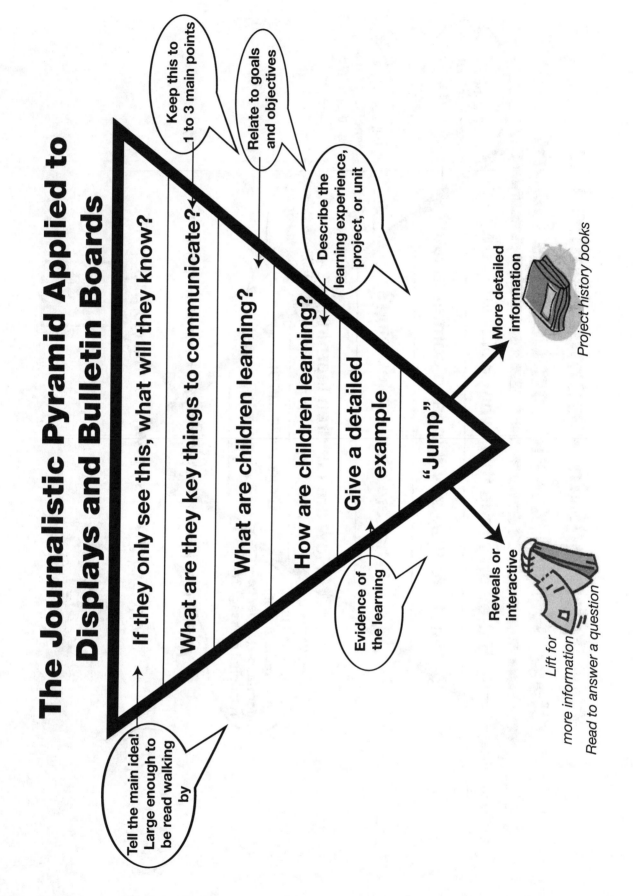

If they only see this, what will they know?

Tell the main idea! Large enough to be read walking by

Keep this to 1 to 3 main points

What are they key things to communicate?

Relate to goals and objectives

What are children learning?

Describe the learning experience, project, or unit

How are children learning?

Give a detailed example

Evidence of the learning

"Jump"

More detailed information

Reveals or interactive

Project history books

Lift for more information

Read to answer a question

References

American Heritage Dictionary of the English Language (4th ed.). (2000). Boston: Houghton Mifflin.

Beneke, S. (1998). *Rearview mirror: Reflections on a preschool car project.* Champaign, IL: ERIC Clearinghouse on Elementary and Early Childhood Education.

Berlo, D. (1960). *The Process of Communication.* New York: Holt, Rinehart, & Winston.

Biagi, S. (2000). *Media/Impact* (5th ed.). Stamford, CT: Wadsworth.

Bureau of Labor Statistics. (2004). *May 2004 national industry-specific occupational employment and wage estimates.* Washington, DC: U.S. Department of Labor.

Cadwell, L. B. (1997). *Bringing Reggio Emilia home: An innovative approach to early childhood education.* New York: Teachers College Press.

Cadwell, L. B. (2003). *Bringing learning to life: A Reggio approach to early childhood education.* New York: Teachers College Press.

Dahlberg, G., Moss, P., & Pence, A. R. (1999). *Beyond quality in early childhood education and care: Postmodern perspectives.* London: Taylor & Francis.

Decker, B. (1991). *You've got to be believed to be heard.* New York: St. Martin's Press.

Dichtelmiller, M. L., Jablon, J. R., Dorfman, A. B., Marsden, D. B., & Meisels, S. J. (1997). *Work sampling in the classroom: A teacher's manual.* Ann Arbor, MI: Rebus.

Donahue, P. L., Finnegan, R. J., Lutkus, A. D., Allen, N. L., & Campbell, J. R. (2000). *The nation's report card: Fourth grade reading 2000* (No. NCES 2001499). Washington, DC: National Center for Education Statistics.

Edwards, C., Gandini, L., & Forman, G. (1998). *The hundred languages of children: The Reggio Emilia approach—advanced reflections* (2nd ed.). Norwood, NJ: Ablex.

Forman, G. (1996). A child constructs an understanding of a water wheel in five media. *Childhood Education, 72*(5), 269–274.

Gandini, L., Hill, L., Cadwell, L., & Schwall, C. (Eds.). (2005). *In the spirit of the studio: Learning from the atelier of Reggio Emilia.* New York: Teachers College Press.

Gardner, H. (1993). *Frames of mind.* New York: Basic Books.

Gronlund, G., & Engel, B. (2001). *Focused portfolios: A complete assessment for the young child.* Saint Paul, MN: Redleaf Press.

Grotta, D., & Grotta, S. W. (2004). *PC Magazine guide to digital photography.* Indianapolis, IN: Wiley.

Gullo, D. F. (2005). *Understanding assessment and evaluation in early childhood education* (2nd ed.). New York: Teachers College Press.

Gurian, E. H.(1996). Noodling around with exhibition opportunities. In G. Durbin (Ed.), *Developing museum exhibitions for lifelong learning* (pp. 3–9). London: Her Majesty's Stationery Office.

Hamilton, C., & Parker, C. (1993). *Communicating for results.* Belmont, CA: Wadsworth.

Helm, A. (1999). *Nonprofit groups and the Kirksville Daily Express: Partners in working for a better community.* Kirksville, MO: Kirksville Daily Express.

Helm, J. H. (2004, September). Projects that power young minds. *Educational Leadership,* pp. 58–62.

Helm, J. H., Beneke, S., & Steinheimer, K. (1997). Documenting children's learning. *Childhood Education, 73*(4), 200–205.

Helm, J. H., Beneke, S., & Steinheimer, K. (1998a). *Teacher materials for documenting children's work.* New York: Teachers College Press.

Helm, J. H., Beneke, S., & Steinheimer, K. (1998b). *Windows on learning: Documenting children's work.* New York: Teachers College Press.

Hertzog, N.B., & Klein, M. M., (2002). Who measures what in our neighborhood? On-line curriculum. The University of Illinois at Urbana-Champaign, Champaign, IL. Retrieved April 13, 2006 from *www.ed.uiuc.edu/ups/curriculum2002/measure/index.shtml.*

Karlins, D. (2004). *PC Magazine guide to printing great digital photos.* Indianapolis, IN: Wiley

Katz, L. G., & Chard, S. C. (1989). *Engaging children's minds: The project approach.* Greenwich, CT: Ablex.

Malaguzzi, L. (1998). History, ideas, and basic philosophy: An interview with Lella Gandini. In L. C. Edwards, L. Gandini, & G. Forman (Eds.), *The hundred languages of children: The Reggio Emilia approach—Advanced reflections* (2nd ed., pp. 41–89). Westwood, CT: Ablex.

Malhotra, N. K. (1982). Information load and consumer decision-making. *Journal of Consumer Research, 8,* 419–430.

McManus, P. (1990). Watch your language! People do read labels. In *What research says about learning in science museums.* Washington, DC: Association of Science-Technology Centers.

Meisels, S. J. (1995). *Performance assessment in early childhood education: The Work Sampling System.* Champaign, IL: ERIC Clearinghouse on Elementary and Early Childhood Education.

Meisels, S. J., Bickel, D. D., Nicholson, J., Hue, Y., Atkins-Burnett, S. (2001). Trusting teachers' judgments: A validity study of a curriculum-embedded performance assessment in kindergarten to grade 3. *American Educational Research Journal, 38*(1) 73–95.

Miles, R., & Tout, A. (1990). Holding power: To choose time

is to save time. In *What research says about learning in science museums*. Washington, DC: Association of Science-Technology Centers.

Morgan, T., & Thaler, S. (1996) *Capturing childhood memories*. New York: Berkley.

Payne, R. K. (2005). *A framework for understanding poverty*. Highlands, TX: Aha! Process.

Petty, R. E., & Cacioppo, J. T. (1981). *Attitudes and persuasion: Classic and contemporary approaches*. Dubuque, IA: Wm. C. Brown.

Rinaldi, C. (2001). Documentation and assessment: What is the relationship? In C. Giudici, C. Rinaldi, & M. Krechevsky (Eds.), *Making learning visible: Children as individual and group learners* (pp. 78–89). Reggio Emilia, Italy: Reggio Children.

Rowan, K. E. (1990). Explaining difficult ideas. In *What research says about learning in science museums*. Washington, DC: Association of Science-Technology Centers.

Snow, C. E., Burns, M. S., & Griffin, P. (1998). *Preventing reading difficulties in young children*. Washington, DC: National Academy Press.

Shorter Oxford English Dictionary. (2002). Oxford, England: Oxford University Press.

Webster's Ninth New Collegiate Dictionary. (1990). Springfield, MA: Merriam-Webster.

Williams, R. (2003). *The non-designers design book* (2nd ed.). Berkeley, CA: Peachpit.

Woodward, E., IV, & Gridina, N. (2000). *Media in the home: The fifth annual survey of parents and children*. Washington, DC: Annenberg Public Policy Center.

Index

About the Authors

Judy Harris Helm, Ed.D., began her career teaching first grade, later going on to teach 4-year-olds, direct and design early childhood programs, and train teachers. She currently assists early childhood and elementary schools in integrating research and new teaching methods through her consulting and training company, Best Practices, Inc. She is past President of the Illinois Association for the Education of Young Children. She is co-author of *Windows on Learning: Documenting Young Children's Work; Teacher Materials for Documenting Children's Work;* Young Investigators: *The Project Approach in the Early Years; The Power of Projects: Meeting Contemporary Challenges in Early Childhood Classrooms;* and *Teaching Your Child to Love Learning: A Guide to Doing Projects at Home.* Dr. Helm served as the primary design consultant for *The Power of Documentation: Children's Learning Revealed,* an exhibit at the Chicago Children's Museum (now a travelling exhibit). Her work has been translated into five languages and she provides consultation and training throughout the country and internationally.

Amanda Helm began her career as a newspaper reporter. She is now an assistant professor of marketing at the University of Wisconsin at Whitewater. She has an M.A. in public relations and advertising and a Ph.D. in marketing. Her undergraduate training is in journalism. Dr. Helm's experiences in the field of communications include university public relations, convention and visitors' bureau, daily newspaper reporting, and newspaper editing. She became interested in the application of marketing and communication skills in education through her involvement with teachers in the Illinois Project Group and Discovery Preschool and her sister, who is a bilingual kindergarten teacher.